A BIBLIOGRAPHY OF MODERN IRISH
AND ANGLO-IRISH LITERATURE

A BIBLIOGRAPHY OF MODERN IRISH AND ANGLO-IRISH LITERATURE

by
Frank L. Kersnowski
C. W. Spinks
Laird Loomis

TRINITY UNIVERSITY PRESS   ●   SAN ANTONIO, TEXAS

This book is dedicated to Harold Orel and Sherman B. Neff

Copyright © by Trinity University Press 1976
Printed in the United States of America
Library of Congress Catalog Card # 75-43274
SBN # 911536-63-9
Printed by Best Printing Company
Bound by Custom Bookbinders

Checklists in the Humanities and Education: A Series

George N. Boyd, Trinity University, Editor

* * * * * *

As a continuing effort, *Checklists in the Humanities and Education: A Series* endeavors to provide the student with essential bibliographical information on important scholarly subjects not readily available in composite form. The series emphasizes selection and limitation of both primary and secondary works, providing a practical and convenient research tool as a primary aim. For example, this bibliography lists primary and secondary material for the main writers of poetry, fiction, and drama in Ireland from 1878 to 1973. Secondary material is confined to book-length critical studies, and material in book-length bibliographies on individual authors is usually not duplicated although books published since the appearance of such bibliographies is included. Likewise, subsequent volumes will remain characteristically selective, limited, and concise.

Checklists in the Humanities and Education: a Series

Harry B. Caldwell, Trinity University, General Editor

English Tragedy, 1370-1600: Fifty Years of Criticism, compiled by Harry B. Caldwell and David L. Middleton

*   *   *   *   *   *

Twentieth-Century Criticism of English Masques, Pageants, and Entertainments: 1558-1642, by David M. Bergeron, with a Supplement on the Folk-Play and Related Forms, by Harry B. Caldwell

*   *   *   *   *   *

Religion in Contemporary Fiction: Criticism from 1945 to the Present, compiled by George N. Boyd and Lois A. Boyd

ACKNOWLEDGMENTS

We are very much indebted to David H. Greene, Roger McHugh, Alf MacLochlainn, Vivian Mercier, Liam Miller, Harold Orel and Dan H. Lawrence for the information and advice they have given us. Without their help, our work would have been less accurate and complete. We also acknowledge the assistance of Austin Clarke, Brian Cleeve, Richard Cary, Helmut Gerber, Edwin Gilcher, Denis Johnston, Thomas Kinsella, John Rees Moore, Richard Murphy, F. G. Stoddard, E. E. Stokes, Jr., and Francis Stuart.

The librarians who helped us overcome time, space, and distance deserve much praise: Dudley B. Ball of the Library of Congress in Washington, D.C.; Deirdre Hamill and W. W. Dieneman of the Library of Trinity College, Dublin; Patrick Henchey and Alf MacLochlainn of the National Library in Dublin; Betty Murphy of the University of Texas in Austin; David Roger of the British Museum in London.

Several bibliographies first appeared elsewhere, wholly, or partially, and are here included with the permission of the editors: Brendan Behan's in *The Hollins Critic* (February, 1965), George Fitzmaurice's in *Irish Writing* (1965), Thomas Kinsella's in the *Dublin Magazine* (Summer, 1966), Brian Moore's in *Critique* (Fall, 1966, and Fall, 1968), and Eimar O'Duffy's in *The Irish Book* (1960).

Those who typed and checked are remembered as invaluable: Katherine McClellan, William H. Spurlock II, Edythe Hirasawa, Lura Wingate, Eva Garza, and Debbie Rattray.

Without the encouragement and financial assistance of the Research Committee of Trinity University this book would still be unfinished.

PREFACE

The writers listed in this bibliography belong to the same culture and are associated with the same literary movement. The culture is Irish, and Donagh McDonagh's definition of the Irish poet in his introduction to *The Oxford Book of Irish Verse* suggests how one may decide who is an Irish writer: "By our definition a poet may be Irish in three ways: by birth, by descent, by adoption." These writers have affirmed, or rebelled from, very similar religious, political, and cultural conditions; have lived in, or exiled themselves from, the same geographical area. All belonged to or were partially inspired by what is called the Irish Literary Renaissance. This period, roughly 1880 to the present, is a time of greatness in Irish literature.

These boundaries of time and culture have been made, as well, by Irish, English, and American scholars. The best works by the Irish are Douglas Hyde's *The Literary History of Ireland* (London: Unwin; New York: Scribner's, 1899), Robert Farren's *The Course of Irish Verse* (London: Sheed and Ward, 1948), Robin Flower's *The Irish Tradition* (Oxford: Clarendon, 1947). American and English presses until recently have issued, in the main, anthologies. David H. Greene's *An Anthology of Irish Literature* (New York: Modern Library, 1954) which has been reissued in 2 vols. (New York: NYU, 1971), Vivian Mercier and David Greene's *1000 Years of Irish Poetry* (New York: Devin-Adair, 1953), and Lennox Robinson and Donagh McDonagh's *The Oxford Book of Irish Verse* (Oxford: Clarendon, 1958) are the most comprehensive. Other useful anthologies are *The Age of Yeats*, ed. George Brandon Saul (New York: Dell, 1964); *The Dolmen Miscellany of Irish Writing*, ed. John Montague and Thomas (Dublin: Dolmen; London and New York:

Oxford, 1962); *The Genius of the Irish Theatre*, ed. Sylvan Barnet, Morton Berman, and William Burton (New York: New American Library, 1941); *Great Irish Short Stories*, ed. Vivian Mercier (New York: Dell, 1964); *Five Great Modern Irish Plays*, ed. George Jean Nathan (New York: Modern Library, 1941); *Irish Stories and Tales* (New York: Devin-Adair, 1955; rev. ed., New York: Washington Square, 1961); *The Mentor Book of Irish Poetry*, ed. Devin A. Garrity (New York: Mentor, 1965); *New Poets of Ireland*, ed. Donald Carroll (Denver: Swallow, 1963); and *The Portable Irish Reader*, ed. Diarmuid Russell (New York: Viking, 1966). Recent American and English publications have added to the critical basis of the study of modern Irish literature. The best of these books are Malcolm Brown's *The Politics of Irish Literature: From Thomas Davis to W. B. Yeats*, Richard J. Loftus's *Nationalism in Modern Anglo-Irish Poetry* (Madison: University of Wisconsin, 1964), Herbert Howarth's *Modern Irish Writers, 1880-1940* (New York: Hill and Wang, 1959), Frank Kersnowski's *The Outsiders: Poets of Contemporary Ireland* (Fort Worth: T.C.U., 1975), and Vivian Mercier's *The Irish Comic Tradition* (London: Oxford, 1960). Other important studies are E. A. Boyd's *Contemporary Drama of Ireland* (Boston: Little, Brown, 1917; Dublin: Talbot; London: Unwin, 1918) and *Ireland's Literary Renaissance* (London and Dublin: Maunsel; New York: Lane, 1916), James Carney's *Studies in Irish Literature and History* (Dublin: Dublin Institute for Advanced Studies, 1955), Brian Cleeve's *Dictionary of Irish Writers*, Vol. I. *Fiction Writers* (Cork: Mercier, 1967), Myles Dillon's *Early Irish Literature* (Chicago: University of Chicago, 1948), Gerard Fay's *The Abbey Theatre. Cradle of Genius* (Dublin: Clonmore and Reynolds, 1958), Una Ellis-Fermor's *The Irish Dramatic Movement* (London: Methuen, 1939), Stephen L. Gwynn's *Irish Literature and Drama in the English Language: A Short History* (London and New York: Nelson, 1936), Maurice Harmon's *Modern Irish Literature, 1800-1967. A Reader's Guide* (Dublin: Dolmen, 1967), Robert Hogan's *After the Renaissance: A Critical History of the Irish Drama Since The Plough and the Stars* (Minneapolis: University of Minnesota, 1967), *Joseph Holloway's Abbey Theatre. A Selection from His Unpublished Journal, Impressions of a Dublin Playgoer*, ed. by Robert Hogan (Carbondale, Ill.: Southern Illinois University, 1967), Brinsley McNamara's *Abbey Plays*, 1899-1948 (Dublin: Sign of the Three Candles, 1949), and Gerald Murphy's *Saga and Myth in Ancient Irish Literature* (Dublin: Colm Ó Lochlainn, 1955). The Irish Writers' Series, edited by James F. Carens and published by Bucknell University Press, provides essential information in monographs, each devoted to a single author. *The Dublin Magazine* and *The University Review* have until recently been the main periodicals for students of

Irish literature. From Belfast came two continuing periodicals: *Threshold*, which began in 1957, and *The Honest Ulsterman*, which began in 1968. In the Republic, *Atlantis* began in 1970. *Studia Hibernica*, published by St. Patrick's Training College in Drumcondra, Dublin, began in 1960. *Hibernica* became an important monthly in 1964. *Eire-Ireland*, published by the Irish American Cultural Institute in St. Paul, Minnesota, began in 1966. Several defunct periodicals are quite important: *Arena* (1963-65), *The Bell* (1940-54), *Envoy* (1949-51), *The Holy Door* (1965), *The Irish Book* (1959-1969), *Poetry Ireland* (1962-1969), and *Rann* (1948-53).

For those who have the language, these critical works in Irish will be important: Frank O'Brien's *Filíocht Ghaeilge na Linne Seo: Staidéar, Criticiúil* (Baile Atha Cliath: An Clochomhar Tta, 1968) and the periodicals *Comhar*, published since 1942 and now edited by Eoghan Ó Hanluain, and *Feasta*, published by the Gaelic League since 1948 and now edited by Aodh Ó Fearghail.

To compile such an extensive bibliography as this, personal taste and bias must be minimized in order that the broadest and most useful listing result. However, all possible inclusions and uses of information are infinite and qualified dissatisfaction of readers seems inevitable. Several writers whom we include might have been rejected by another compiler because they have, except for birth, scant associations with Ireland. Joyce Cary, Cecil Day Lewis, Lawrence Durrell, and Robert Graves are the most noticeable examples. We have chosen to include them for two reasons: (1) because commission seems a lesser offense than omission, and (2) because these writers illustrate the difficulty of limiting Irish literature to the self-conscious Celticism of Yeats and Joyce.

Usually, we have included writers because they figure so significantly in anthologies and critical studies that they are unavoidable. Some writers, such as Denis Devlin, Brian O'Nolan, and Brian Moore, who have not yet won a place, we include because we are convinced of their worth. Some writers we have included because scholars who read this manuscript are convinced of their worth. Exclusions, of course, exist. We list here writers who at a later date or to another compiler may seem as unavoidable or irresistible as those of our own choosing: Monk Gibbon, Emily Lawless, Brinsley McNamara, Edna O'Brien, Iris Murdoch, George Sigerson, and Jack B. Yeats. In all cases, we have chosen writers who were essentially creative rather than scholarly or critical and who wrote more in English than Irish. We have excluded L. A. G. Strong and John Eglinton (W. K. Magee) because they wrote mainly memoirs. At times, we have excluded writers of interest because they have not yet published much.

Striving to strike a medium between a checklist of titles and a descriptive bibliography, we have not mentioned half-titles, dedications, and acknowledgments; but we have listed any introductory material or notes, as well as the size of editions when possible. We include all collected and selected works, first editions or individual titles, revised and enlarged editions, books edited or translated by the writers, books for which the writers wrote introductory material, and book-length critical studies about the writers themselves. We do not include translations made by anyone other than the writer, broadsheets, broadsides, recordings, or sheet music. Except for a few unusual items, we have cited only books published by Irish, English, and American houses.

If an adequate bibliography has appeared in book form, we refer to it rather than duplicate its entries, but we do list any books by a writer which have been published since the bibliography was compiled. We list secondary material when necessary. If a bibliography appeared in a periodical, we reprint it here; the two exceptions are the continuing bibliographies of works about Shaw in the *Shaw Review* and the one about Joyce in the *James Joyce Quarterly*, necessitating a selective bibliography for both. For Shaw's own writings, as well, we have given a selection, made with the help of Dan H. Lawrence. Such extensive bibliographies need to be published independently.

The period of time we have tried to cover extends from 1878 through 1973. An asterisk before an entry indicates that we have not seen the book. Information given as a calculated guess is enclosed in brackets. We have retained any punctuation in the published title.

TABLE OF CONTENTS

A BIBLIOGRAPHY OF MODERN IRISH
AND ANGLO-IRISH LITERATURE

Samuel Beckett (1906-   )

STANDARD BIBLIOGRAPHY

Federman, Raymond and Fletcher, John. *Samuel Beckett: His Work and His Critics.* Berkeley and Los Angeles: University of California, 1970.

BIBLIOGRAPHY OF CRITICISM

Tanner, James T. F. and Vann, J. Don. *Samuel Beckett: A Checklist of Criticism.* Kent: Kent State University, 1969.

COLLECTED WORKS

Collected Works, 16 vols. New York: Grove, 1970 (reg. and signed ltd. ed.).

PLAYS

Collected Plays. 2 vols. In English, German and French. Frankfurt, Germany: Adler's Foreign Books, n.d.

Breath and Other Shorts. London: Faber and Faber, 1971.

Cascando and Other Short Dramatic Pieces. New York: Grove, 1969.

Film (a film script). New York: Grove, 1969. Complete scenario, il, production shots; with an essay on directing film by Alan Schneider.

Not I. London: Faber and Faber; New York: Grove, 1973.

Theater of the Absurd: An Anthology. New York: Grove, 1974.

PROSE

First Love and Other Shorts. New York: Grove, 1974.

*Hiniveis auf Pim. Mit 10 Radierungen von Manfred Garstka. (Köln) Hake (1966).

Lessness. London: Calder and Boyars, 1970.

The Lost Ones. (Originally published as *Le Depeupleur,* Les Editions de Minuit, Paris, 1971). London: Calder & Boyars; New York: Grove, 1972.

Mercier and Camier. Trans. from the original French by the author. New York: Grove, 1974.

*Mercier et Camier. Paris: Les Editions de minuit, 1970.

The North. With three etchings by Avigdor Arikha. London: Enitharmon, 1972. Limited signed edition.

TRANSLATION

Bosquet, Alain. *Selected Poems.* Translated from French by: Wallace Fowlie, Lawrence Durrell, Samuel Beckett, Jean and Elisabeth Malaquais. Athens, Ohio: Ohio University, 1973.

BIOGRAPHY & CRITICISM

Abbott, H. Porter. *The Fiction of Samuel Beckett: Form and Effect.* Berkeley, Calif: University of California, 1973.

Alvarez, A. *Samuel Beckett.* New York: Viking, 1973.

Barnard, G. C. *Samuel Beckett: A New Approach.* New York: Dodd, Mead, 1970.

Chevigny, Bell Gale, editor. *Twentieth Century Interpretations of Endgame.* Englewood Cliffs, New Jersey: Prentice-Hall, 1969.

Cohn, Ruby H. *Back to Beckett.* Princeton, New Jersey: Princeton University, 1974.

Doherty, Francis. *Samuel Beckett.* London: Hutchinson, 1971.

Duckworth, Colin. *Angels of Darkness: Dramatic Effect in Samuel Beckett with Special Reference to Eugene Ionesco.* New York: Barnes & Noble, 1972.

Fletcher, John and Spurling, John. *Beckett: A Study of His Plays*. New York: Hill & Wang, 1972.

Friedman, Melvin, Jr., editor. *Samuel Beckett Now: Critical Approaches to His Novels, Poetry and Plays*. Chicago: University of Chicago, 1970.

Hart, Clive. *Samuel Beckett*. (Irish Writers Series). Lewisburg, Pa.: Bucknell University, [n.d.].

Harvey, Lawrence E. *Samuel Beckett: Poet and Critic*. Princeton, New Jersey: Princeton University, 1970.

Hayman, Ronald. *Samuel Beckett*. New York: Ungar, 1973.

Hesla, David H. *Shape of Chaos: An Interpretation of the Art of Samuel Beckett*. Minneapolis: University of Minnesota, 1971.

Kennedy, Sighle. *Murphy's Bed*. Lewisburg, Pa.: Bucknell University, 1971.

Kenner, Hugh. *A Reader's Guide to Samuel Beckett*. New York: Farrar, Straus, and Giroux, 1973.

Kern, Edith. *Existential Thought and Fictional Technique: Kierkegaard, Sartre, Beckett*. New Haven, Conn.: Yale University, 1970.

O'Hara, James Donald, editor. *Twentieth Century Interpretations of Molloy, Malone Dies, The Unnameable*. Englewood Cliffs, New Jersey: Prentice-Hall, 1970.

Robinson, Michael. *Long Sonata of the Dead: A Study of Samuel Beckett*. New York: Grove, 1969.

Schlossberg, Edwin. *Einstein and Beckett. A record of an imaginary discussion with Albert Einstein and Samuel Beckett*, by Edwin Schlossberg. Foreword by John Unterecker. New York: Links, 1973.

Schulz, Hans-Joachim. *This Hell of Stories—A Hegelian Approach to the Novels of Samuel Beckett*. The Hague: Mouton, 1973.

Sen, Supti. *Samuel Beckett: His Mind and Art*. Calcutta: Firma K. L. Mukhopadhyay, 1970.

Szanto, George Herbert. *Narrative Consciousness: Structure and Perception in the Fiction of Kafka, Beckett and Robbe-Grillet*. Austin, Texas: University of Texas, 1972.

Via, Dan O. *Commentary on Samuel Beckett's Waiting for Godot*. Lee Belford, editor. (Religious Dimensions in Literature Series). New York: Seabury, [n.d.]

Webb, Eugene. *Samuel Beckett: A Study of His Novels.* Seattle: University of Washington, 1970.

Brendan Behan (1923-1964)

PLAYS

Brendan Behan's Borstal Boy. Adapted for the stage by Frank McMahon. New York: Random House, 1971.

The Hostage. London: Methuen; New York: Grove, 1958. Rev. ed., London: Methuen, 1962.

Moving Out and A Garden Party. Two plays. Intro. by Micheál Ó hAodaha. Ed. by Robert Hogan. Dixon, Calif.: Proscenium, 1967.

The Quare Fellow. A comedy-drama. London: Methuen, 1956. New York: Grove, c1956, 1957.

The Quare Fellow and The Hostage. Two Plays. New York: Grove, 1964.

FICTION

Hold Your Hour and Have Another. London: Hutchinson, 1963. Boston: Little, Brown, c1963, 1964.

The Scarperer. Garden City, N.Y.: Doubleday, 1964. London: Hutchinson, 1966.

NON-FICTION

Borstal Boy. London: Hutchinson, 1958. New York: Knopf, 1959.

Brendan Behan's Island: An Irish Sketch-Book. (Drawings by Paul Hogarth). New York: Geis Associates, dist. by Random House; London: Hutchinson, 1962.

Brendan Behan's New York. (Drawings by Paul Hogarth). New York: Geis Associates, dist. by Random House; London: Hutchinson, 1964.

Confessions of an Irish Rebel. London: Hutchinson, 1965. New York: Geis Associates, dist. by Random House, c1965, 1966.

The Wit of Brendan Behan. Compiled by Sean McCann. London: Leslie Frewin, 1968.

CRITICAL AND BIOGRAPHICAL STUDIES

Behan, Dominic. *My Brother Brendan.* New York: Simon and Schuster, c1965, 1966.

Boyle, Ted E. *Brendan Behan.* New York: Twayne, 1969.

*Jeffs, R. *Brendan Behan: Man and Showman.* London: Hutchinson, 1966. Cleveland: World Publishing, 1968.

McCann, Sean (ed.). *The World of Brendan Behan.* London: New English Library, 1965.

O'Connor, Ulick. *Brendan Behan.* London: Hamilton, 1970.

Porter, Raymond J. *Brendan Behan.* New York: Columbia University, 1973.

Simpson, Alan. *Beckett and Behan; and a theatre in Dublin.* London: Routledge and Paul, 1962.

Elizabeth Bowen (1899-1973)

COLLECTED WORKS

The Collected (Uniform) Edition. London: Cape, 1948–.

The Cat Jumps; and other stories. 1949.

The Death of the Heart. 1948.

The Demon Lover; and other stories. 1952.

Friends and Relations. 1951.

The Heat of the Day. 1954.

The Hotel. 1950.

The House in Paris. 1949.

Joining Charles; and other stories. 1952.

The Last September. 1948.

Look at All Those Roses. 1951.

To the North. 1950.

Pictures and Conversations. Foreword by Spencer Curtis Brown. New York: Knopf, 1975.

COLLECTED STORIES

Ann Lee's; and Other Stories. London: Sidgwick and Jackson, 1926. New York: Boni and Liveright, 1928.

The Cat Jumps. London: Gollancz, 1934.

A Day in the Dark; and Other Stories. London: Cape, 1965.

The Demon Lover; and Other Stories. London: Cape, 1946. Pub. in USA with title *Ivy Gripped the Steps; and Other Stories.* New York: Knopf, 1946.

Early Stories. New York: Knopf, c1950, 1951. First pub. as *Encounters and Ann Lee's.*

Encounters. Stories. London: Sidgwick and Jackson; New York: Boni and Liveright, 1923. Same with pref. and title Early Stories. London: Sidgwick and Jackson, 1949.

Ivy Gripped the Steps. See *The Demon Lover.*

Joining Charles; and Other Stories. London: Constable; New York: Dial, 1929.

Look at All Those Roses. Short stories. London: Gollancz; New York: Knopf, 1941.

Selected Stories. Dublin and London: Fridberg, 1946.

Stories by Elizabeth Bowen. New York: Vintage, 1959.

COLLECTED NON-FICTION

Afterthought. Pieces about writing. Fore. London: Longmans, Green, 1962.

Collected Impressions. London: Longmans, Green; New York: Knopf, 1950.

NOVELS

The Death of the Heart. London: Gollancz; New York: Knopf, 1939.

Eva Trout; or, changing scenes. New York: Knopf, 1968.

Friends and Relations: A novel. London: Constable; New York: Dial, 1931.

The Good Tiger. New York: Knopf, 1965.

The Heat of the Day. London: Cape; New York: Knopf, c1948, 1949.

The Hotel. London: Constable, 1927. New York: Dial, 1928.

The House in Paris. London: Gollancz, 1935. New York: Knopf, c1935, 1936.

The Last September. London: Constable; New York: Dial, 1929. Same with a pref. by Elizabeth Bowen. New York: Knopf, 1952.

The Little Girls. London: Cape; New York: Knopf, 1964.

A Time in Rome. New York: Knopf, c1959, 1960. London: Longmans, Green, 1960.

To the North. London: Gollancz, 1932. New York: Knopf, c1932, 1933.

A World of Love. London: Cape; New York: Knopf, 1955.

NON-FICTION

Bowen's Court: An account of the Bowen family. London: Longmans, Green; New York: Knopf, 1942.

English Novelists. London: Collins, 1942.

Seven Winters. Dublin: Cuala, 1942. 450 numbered copies. Same with title *Seven Winters: Memories of a Dublin childhood*. London, New York, and Toronto: Longmans, Green, 1943.

Seven Winters: Memories of a Dublin childhood. And After-Thoughts. Pieces on writing. New York: Knopf, 1962.

The Shelbourne: A centre in Dublin life for more than a century. London: Harrap, 1951. Pub. in the USA with title *The Shelbourne Hotel*. New York: Knopf, 1951.

PLAY

Anthony Trollope. A new judgement. London and New York: Oxford, 1946.

JOINT AUTHOR

With Graham Greene and V. S. Pritchett. *Why Do I Write? An exchange of views*. Pref. by V. S. Pritchett. London: Marshal, 1948.

With others. *Family Christmas Book*. Ed. Dorothy Wilson. London: Bailey; New York: Prentice Hall, 1957.

With others. *How I Write My Novels*. Comp. John Irwin. Coll. and prod. for the B.B.C. television magazine programme Kaleidoscope. Ed. Ted James. London: Spearman, 1948.

EDITED

Austen, Jane, *Pride and Prejudice*. Intro. London: Williams and Norgate, 1948.

The Faber Book of Modern Stories. Intro. London: Faber and Faber, 1937.

Heppenstall, Rayner. *Blaze of Noon*. London: Secker and Warburg, 1939. Chicago: Alliance, 1940.

Le Fanu, Joseph S. *Uncle Silas: A tale of Bartram-Haugh*. Intro. London: Cresset, 1947.

Mansfield, Katherine. *Stories*. Intro. New York: Vintage, 1956. London and Glasgow: Collins, 1957.

Ruskin, John. *The King of the Golden River; or, The Black Brothers*. Intro. London and New York: Macmillan, 1962.

Trollope, Anthony. *Doctor Thorne*. Intro. New York: Houghton, 1959.

BIOGRAPHICAL AND CRITICAL STUDIES

Austin, Allan E. *Elizabeth Bowen*. New York: Twayne, 1971.

Brooke, Jocelyn. *Elizabeth Bowen*. London, New York and Toronto: Pub. for the British Book League and the National Book League by Longmans, Green, 1952.

Heath, William Webster. *Elizabeth Bowen: An Introduction to Her Novels*. Madison: University of Wisconsin, 1961.

Kenney, Edwin J. *Elizabeth Bowen:* (Irish Writers Series.) Lewisburg, Pa.: Bucknell University [n. d.].

Shan F. Bullock, pseud. of John William Bullock (1865-1935)

FICTION

The Awkward Squads; and other stories. London: Cassell, 1893.

The Barrys. London: Harper; New York and London: Doubleday and McClure, 1899.

By Thrasna River: The Story of a townland. London: Ward, Lock, and Bowden, 1895.

The Charmer: A seaside comedy. London: Bowden, 1897.

The Cubs: The story of a friendship. London: Laurie, 1906.

Dan the Dollar. Dublin: Maunsel [1905].

Hetty: The story of an Ulster family. London: Laurie [1911].

Irish Pastorals. London: Grant Richards; New York: McClure, Phillips, 1901.

A Laughing Matter. London: Laurie [1908].

The Loughsiders. London, Calcutta, Sydney: Harrap; New York: Dial, 1924.

Master John. London: Laurie [1909].

Mr. Ruby Jumps the Traces. London: Chapman and Hall, 1917.

The Red Leaguers. London: Methuen; New York: McClure, Phillips, 1904.

Ring o' Rushes. London: Ward, Lock, and Bowden; New York: Stone and Kimball, 1896.

Rogue Bartley. Chicago: Stone and Kimball, 1896.

The Splendid Shilling. Chicago: Stone and Kimball, 1896.

The Squireen. London: Methuen; New York: McClure, Phillips, 1903.

NON-FICTION

After Sixty Years. Fore. by Sir Horace Plunkett. London: Low [1931].

Robert Thorne: The story of a London clerk. Introductory note. London: Laurie [1907].

Thomas Andrews: Shipbuilder. Intro. by Sir Horace Plunkett. Dublin and London: Maunsel, 1912. Same with title *A "Titanic" Hero. Thomas Andrews. Shipbuilder.* Baltimore: Norman, Remington, 1913.

POETRY

Gleanings: Verses. Sutton: Pile [1926].

Mors et Vita: Poems. Fore. by AE. London: Laurie, 1923. 350 copies.

JOINT AUTHOR

With Emily Lawless. *The Race of Castlebar. Being a narrative addressed by Mr. John Bunbury to his brother Mr. Theodore Bunbury, attached to His Britannic Majesty's Embassy at Florence, October 1798.* London: Murray, 1913.

Joseph Campbell, pseud.
Seosamh MacCathmhaoil (1879-1944)

POETRY

COLLECTED POEMS

The Poems of Joseph Campbell. Ed. with an intro. by Austin Clarke. Dublin: Figgis, 1963.

INDIVIDUAL TITLES

Earth of Cualann. With twenty-one designs by the author. Dublin and London: Maunsel, 1917. 500 numbered copies.

The Garden of the Bees; and other poems. Decor. by the author. Dublin: Gill; Belfast: Mayne [1905].

The Gilly of Christ. Dublin: Maunsel, 1907.

The Man Child. Introductory note. Being No. 1 of the Loch Press Series of Booklets: March, 1907. [Dublin]: n.p., 1907.

The Mountainy Singer. Dublin: Maunsel, 1909. Boston: Four Seas, 1910.

The Rush-light. Poems. Dublin: Maunsel, 1906.

PROSE AND PLAYS

Irishry. Pref. Dublin and London: Maunsel [1913].

Judgement. A play in two acts. Dublin and London: Maunsel, 1912.

Mearing Stones. Leaves from my note-book on tramp in Donegal. With sixteen pencil drawings by the author. Dublin: Maunsel, 1911.

JOINT AUTHOR

Campbell, Nancy. *Agnus Dei.* Illus. by Joseph Campbell. Dublin: Maunsel, 1920.

With Sir Hamilton Harty. *Three Traditional Ulster Airs.* The words by Seosamh MacCathmhaoil. Arr. by Hamilton Harty. London: Boosey, 1905.

With Herbert Hughes. *Songs of Uladh.* Coll. and arr. by Padraic Mac-Aodh O Neill, *i.e.,* Herbert Hughes. With words by Seosamh Mac-Cathmhaoil and Designs by Seaghan MacCathmhaoil. Dublin: Gill; Belfast: Mullen, 1904.

With Annie D. Scott. *Four Irish Songs.* The words by Joseph Campbell. The Music by Annie D. Scott. London: Boosey, 1910.

TRANSLATED BY

Pearse, Patrick Henry. *The Collected Works of Padraic H. Pearse.* Vol. 1. *Plays, Stories, Poems.* Intro. by Patrick Brown. Dublin and London: Maunsel; New York: Stokes, 1917. The stories alone are trans. by Campbell.

——. *Iosagan; and other stories.* Dublin: Maunsel, 1918.

BIBLIOGRAPHY

O'Hegarty, Patrick Sarsfield. *A Bibliography of Joseph Campbell.* Dublin: Pvt. ptd. by Thom, 1940. 35 copies.

Joyce Cary (1888-1957)

COLLECTED AND SELECTED WORKS

The Carfax Edition. Each novel with a preface by the author. London: Joseph, 1951.

The African Witch. 1951.

Aissa Saved. 1952.

An American Visitor. 1952.

The Captive and the Free. 1963.

Castle Corner. 1952.

Charley Is My Darling. 1951.

A Fearful Joy. 1952.

Herself Surprised. 1951.

The Horse's Mouth. 1951.

A House of Children. 1951.

Mister Johnson. 1952.

The Moonlight. 1952.

Not Honour More. 1966.

Prisoner of Grace. 1954.

To Be A Pilgrim. 1951.

First Trilogy: Herself Surprised, To Be A Pilgrim and The Horse's Mouth. With a preface by Joyce Cary. New York: Harper, 1958.

Spring Song; and other stories. London: Joseph; New York: Harper, 1960.

INDIVIDUAL WORKS

The African Witch. London: Gollancz; New York: Morrow, 1936.

Aissa Saved. London: Benn, 1932. New York: Harper, 1963.

An American Visitor. London: Benn, 1933. New York: Harper, 1961.

The Captive and the Free. London: Joseph; New York: Harper, 1959.

Castle Corner. London: Gollancz, 1938. New York and Evanston: Harper, 1963.

Charley Is My Darling. London: Joseph, 1940. New York: Harper, 1959.

*Cock Jarvis. A. G. Bishop, editor. London: Joseph, 1974.

Except the Lord. London: Joseph; New York: Harper, 1953.

A Fearful Joy. London: Joseph; New York: Harper, 1949. Same with a pref. by Cary. Garden City, New York: Doubleday, 1961.

Herself Surprised. London: Joseph; New York: Harper, 1941. Same with a note by Andrew Wright. New York: Harper, 1961.

The Horse's Mouth. London: Joseph; New York: Harper, 1944. Same with a note by Andrew Wright. New York: Harper, 1959. Same with a self-portrait and eight illus. by the author and *The Old Strife at Plant's*, a discarded chapter of *The Horse's Mouth*. Ed. by Andrew Wright with pref., notes, and bibliography. Oxford: At the New Bodleian, 1956.

A House of Children. London: Joseph, 1941. New York: Harper [1956].

Mister Johnson. London: Gollancz, 1939. New York: Harper [1951].

The Moonlight. London: Joseph; New York and London: Harper, 1946.

Not Honour More. London: Joseph; New York: Harper, 1955.

Prisoner of Grace. London: Joseph; New York: Harper, 1952.

To Be A Pilgrim. London: Joseph; New York: Harper, 1942.

POETRY

The Drunken Sailor. Illus. by Joyce Cary. London: Joseph, 1947.

Marching Soldier. London: Joseph, 1945.

Verse by Arthur Cary. Edinburgh: Robert Grant, 1908.

POLITICAL AND CRITICAL PROSE

Art and Reality. Cambridge: Cambridge University; New York: Harper, 1958.

*Chapters XIX and XX from Art and Reality, Ways of Creative Process. Kalamazoo: Sequoia, 1965.

Britain and West Africa. London, New York, and Toronto: Longmans, Green, 1946. Same with new appendix in 1947.

The Case for African Freedom. London: Secker and Warburg, 1941. Rev. and enl. ed. London: Secker and Warburg, 1944.

The Case for African Freedom; and other writings on Africa. Intro. by Christopher Fyfe. Austin: University of Texas, 1962.

Memoir of the Bobotes. Fore. by Walter Allen. London: Joseph [1960]. Same with intro. by James B. Meriwether. Illus. by the author. Austin: University of Texas, 1960.

Power in Men. London: Nicholson and Watson, 1939. Same with an intro. by Hazard Adams. Seattle: University of Washington, 1963.

Process of Real Freedom. London: Joseph, 1943.

BIOGRAPHICAL AND CRITICAL STUDIES

Allen, Walter E. *Joyce Cary*. London: Pub. by Longmans, Green for the British Council and National Book League, 1953. Writers and Their Work, No. 41. Rev. ed., 1954.

Bloom, Robert. *The Indeterminate World: A Study of the novels of Joyce Cary*. Philadelphia: University of Pennsylvania; London: Oxford, 1962.

Echeruo, Michael. *Joyce Cary and the Novel of Africa*. London: Longmans; New York: Africana, 1973.

Hoffman, Charles G. *Joyce Cary: The Comedy of Freedom*. Pittsburgh: University of Pittsburgh, 1964.

Larsen, Golden L. *The Dark Descent: Social Change and Moral Responsibility in the Novels of Joyce Cary*. London: Joseph, 1965.

Mahood, Molly M. *Joyce Cary's Africa*. London: Methuen, 1964.

Noble, Robert W. *Joyce Cary*. Edinburgh: Oliver and Boyd; New York: Barnes and Noble, 1973.

*Wolkenfeld, Jack. *Joyce Cary: The Developing Style*. New York: New York University, 1968.

Wright, Andrew. *Joyce Cary: A Preface to his Novels*. New York: Harper; London: Chatto and Windus; Toronto: Irwin and Clark, 1958.

Austin Clarke (1896-1974)

STANDARD BIBLIOGRAPHY

Miller, Liam. "The Books of Austin Clarke. A Checklist," *A Tribute to Austin Clarke on his Seventieth Birthday*. Ed. by Liam Miller and John Montague. Dublin: Dolmen, 1966.

POEMS

Collected Poems. Ed. by Liam Miller. Illustrated by Bernard Childs. Dublin: Dolmen; London: Oxford University, 1974.

The Echo at Coole; and other poems. Dublin: Dolmen, 1968.

Old-Fashioned Pilgrimage; and other poems. Dublin: Dolmen, 1967.

A Sermon on Swift; and other poems. Templeogue: Bridge, 1968. 250 copies.

PROSE

The Celtic Twilight and the Nineties. Ed. by George Crabbe. Dublin: Dolmen, 1969; Harmondsworth: Penguin, 1973.
A Penny in the Clouds: More Memories of Ireland and England. London: Routledge and Kegan Paul, 1968.

PLAYS

Two Interludes adapted from Cervantes: The Student from Salamanca, 'La Cueva de Salamanca,' and The Silent Lover, 'El Viejo Celoso.' Dublin: Dolmen, c1966, 1968.

BIOGRAPHY AND CRITICISM

Halpern, Susan. *Austin Clarke: His Life and Works.* Dublin: Dolmen; New York: Humanties Press, 1974.

Padraic Colum (1881-1972)

FICTION

Big Tree of Bunlahy. Stories of my own countryside. New York, London, and Toronto: Macmillan, 1933.

Boy Apprenticed to an Enchanter. New York: Macmillan, 1920.
A Boy in Eirinn. London: Dent; New York: Dutton, 1913. Rev. ed. by Dutton in 1929.

Boy Who Knew What the Birds Said. New York: Macmillan, 1918.

Castle Conquer. New York: Macmillan, 1923.

Children Who Followed the Piper. New York: Macmillan, 1922.

The Flying Swans. New York: Crown, 1957.

Forge in the Forest. New York: Macmillan, 1925.

Fountain of Youth; Stories to be told. New York: Macmillan, 1927. Dublin: Educational Co. of Ireland, 1939.

Girl Who Sat by the Ashes. New York: Macmillan, 1919.

The King of Ireland's Son. New York: Holt, 1916. London: Harrap, 1920.

The Peep-Show Man. New York: Macmillan, 1924.

Six Who Were Left in a Shoe. Chicago: Volland, 1923.

Story Telling New and Old. New York: Macmillan, 1961.

Where the Winds Never Blew and the Cocks Never Crew. New York and Toronto: Macmillan, 1940.

White Sparrow. New York: Macmillan, 1933.

PLAYS

Balloon: A comedy in four acts. New York: Macmillan, 1929.

The Desert: A play in three acts. Dublin: Devereux, Newth, 1912.

The Fiddler's House: A play in three acts. Dublin: Maunsel, 1907.

The Fiddler's House, a play in three acts, and The Land, an agrarian comedy. Dublin: Maunsel, 1909.

The Land. Dublin: Maunsel; New York: n.p., 1905. New York ed. of 100 numbered copies.

Mogu the Wanderer; or, the desert. A fantastic comedy in three acts. Boston: Little, Brown, 1917.

Moytura: A play for dancers. Dublin: Dolmen, 1963.

Studies. Dublin: Maunsel, 1907.

Thomas Muskery: A play in three acts. Dublin: Maunsel, 1910. Boston: Luce, n.d.

Three Plays: The Fiddler's House, The Land, Thomas Muskery. Boston: Little, Brown, 1916. Rev. ed., New York: Macmillan, 1925; Dublin: Figgis, 1963.

POETRY

Collected Poems. New York: Devin-Adair, 1953.

Creatures. New York: Macmillan, 1927.

Dramatic Legends; and other poems. London and New York: Macmillan, 1922.

Flower Pieces: New Poems. Dublin: Orwell, 1938. 300 numbered copies.

Fourteen Stations of the Cross. Chicago: Seymour, n.d.

Heather Ale: A book of verses. Dublin: n.d., 1907.

Images of Departure. Dublin: Dolmen, 1969.

Irish Elegies. Dublin: Dolmen, 1958. Rev. ed., 1961.

Jackdaw. Dublin: Gayfield, 1919.

Old Pastures. Note. New York: Macmillan, 1930.

Poems. London and New York: Macmillan, 1932.

Songs from Connacht: Nine poems by Padraic Colum, set to music by Herbert Hughes. London: Boosey, 1913.

The Story of Lowry Maen. Pref. New York: Macmillan, 1937.

Ten Poems. Dublin: Dolmen, 1957. 50 copies.

Vegetable Kingdom. Bloomington: Indiana University, 1954.

Wild Earth: A book of verse. Dublin: Maunsel, 1907. Rev. and enl. ed., Wild Earth; and other poems. Dublin: Maunsel; New York: Holt, 1916. Rev. and enl. ed., Wild Earth. Poems. Dublin: Talbot, 1950.

TALES AND LEGENDS

Adventures of Odysseus and The Tale of Troy. New York: Macmillan, 1918. London: Harrap, 1920.

At the Gateway of the Day: Tales and Legends of Hawaii, vol. I. New Haven: Pub. for the Hawaiian Legend and Folklore Commission by the Yale University Press, 1924.

The Bright Islands: Tales and Legends of Hawaii, vol. II. New Haven: Pub. for the Hawaiian Legend and Folklore Commission by the Yale University Press; London: Milford, 1925.

Children of Odin. New York: Macmillan, 1920. London: Harrap, 1922.

Children's Homer: The adventures of Odysseus and The Tale of Troy. New York: Macmillan, 1918.

Frenzied Prince: Being heroic stories of ancient Ireland. New York: McKay, 1943.

The Golden Fleece; and the heroes who lived before Achilles. New York: Macmillan, 1921.

The Island of the Mighty: Being the hero stories of Celtic Britain retold from the Mabinogion. New York: Macmillan, 1924.

Legend of St. Columbia. New York: Macmillan, 1935. London: Sheed, Ward; New York: Oxford University, 1936.

Legends of Hawaii. New Haven: Yale University; London: Milford, 1937.

Myths of the World. See *Orpheus; Myths of the world.*

Orpheus: Myths of the world. New York: Macmillan, 1930. 350 numbered copies.

The Stone of Victory; and other tales. Fore. by Virginia Haviland. New York: McGraw-Hill, 1966.

Story-Telling New and Old. New York: Macmillan, 1968. Signed by Colum and Artzybasheff (illustrator). Same with title *Myths of the World.* New York: Grosset and Dunlap, 1959.

The Voyagers: Being legends and romances of Atlantic discovery. New York: Macmillan, 1925.

TRAVEL BOOKS

Cross Roads in Ireland. London and New York: Macmillan, 1930.

A Half-day's Ride; or, Estates in Corsica. London and New York: Macmillan, 1932.

My Irish Year. London: Mills and Boon; New York: Pott, 1912.

The Road Round Ireland. Pref. New York: Macmillan, 1926.

LETTERS

Cabell, James Branch. *Between Friends: Letters of the author and others.* Ed. by Padraic Colum and Margaret Freeman Cabell with an intro. by Carl van Vechen. New York: Harcourt, 1962.

JOINT AUTHOR

With Mary Colum. *Our Friend James Joyce.* New York: Doubleday, 1958. London: Gollancz, 1959.

BIOGRAPHICAL

Ourselves Alone! The story of Arthur Griffith and the origin of the Irish Free State. Intro. by Crane Brinton. New York: Crown, 1959. Same without intro. and with title *Arthur Griffith*. Dublin: Brown and Nolan, 1959.

Three Men. London: Mathews and Marot, 1930. 530 numbered and signed copies.

EDITED AND INTRODUCTION BY

Anthology of Irish Verse: The poetry of Ireland from Mythological times to the present. Intro. New York: Boni and Liveright, 1922. Rev. and enl. ed., 1948.

The Arabian Nights: Tales of wonder and magnificence. New York: Macmillan, 1923.

Barkentin, Marjorie. *James Joyce's Ulysses in Nighttown: Dramatized and transposed by Marjorie Barkentin under the supervision of Padraic Colum*. Fore. New York: Random House, 1958.

Between Friends. See Letters.

Broadsheet Ballads: Being a collection of Irish popular songs. Intro. and notes. Dublin and London: Maunsel [1913]. Baltimore: Remington, 1917.

Clarke, Austin. *Collected Poems*. Intro. London: Allen and Unwin, 1936.

Cromwell, Gladys. *Poems*. Intro. New York: Macmillan, 1919.

Denson, Alan. *Printed Writings by George Russell (AE). A bibliography with some notes on his pictures and portraits*. Fore. Reminiscences of AE by M. J. Bonn. A note on AE and painting by Thomas Bodkin. Evanston and London: Northwestern University, 1961.

Lord Dunsany. *A Dreamer's Tales; and other stories*. Intro. New York: Boni and Liveright, 1919.

Ferguson, Sir Samuel. *Poems of Samuel Ferguson*. Ed. with an intro. Dublin: Hodges, 1963.

Goldsmith, Oliver. *Essays, Poems, Letters, and Plays*. Arr., sel., with appreciation. Dublin: Talbot [1928].

——. *Oliver Goldsmith*. Intro. London: Daniel [1913].

——. *The Vicar of Wakefield: A tale supposedly written by himself*. Intro. New York: Collier, 1963.

Griffin, Gerald. *The Collegians*. Intro. Dublin: Talbot [1918].

Joyce, James. *Anna Livia Plurabelle*. Pref. New York: Gaige, 1928. 800 signed and numbered copies.

——. *Dubliners*. Intro. New York: Random House [1954].

——. *Exiles: A play in three acts including hitherto unpub. notes by the author, discovered after his death*. Intro. London: Cape, 1952. New York: Viking, 1961.

MacKenna, Stephen. *Journal and Letters*. Ed. with a memoir by E. R. Dodds. Pref. London: Constable, 1936.

Nic Shiubhlaigh, Maire. *The Splendid Years: Recollections of Maire Nic Shiublaigh as told to Edward Kenny*. With appendices and lists of Irish Theatre plays, 1899-1916. Fore. Dublin: Duffy, 1955.

With Edward O'Brien. *Poems of the Irish Revolutionary Brotherhood: Thomas MacDonagh, P. H. Pearse (Padráic Mac Piarais), Joseph Mary Plunkett, Sir Roger Casement*. Boston: Small, Maynard, July 1916. Enl. ed., Sept. 1916.

Ohta, Takashi and Margaret Sperry. *The Golden Wind*. Intro. London: Cape, 1930.

O'Sullivan, Seumas (pseud. of James Starkey). *Poems of Seumas O'Sullivan*. Intro. Boston: Brimmer, 1923.

Poe, Edgar Allan. *Edgar Allan Poe's Tales of Mystery and Imagination*. Intro. London: Dent; New York: Dutton [1908].

The Poet's Circuits: Collected poems of Ireland. London: Oxford, 1960.

Roofs of Gold: Poems to be read aloud. Ed. with an intro. London: Collier; New York: Macmillan, 1964.

Sigerson, George. *Songs and Poems*. Intro. Dublin: Duffy, 1927.

Stephens, James. *James Stephens: A selection*. Sel. with an intro. by Lloyd Frankenburg. Pref. London: Macmillan, 1962. Same pub. in the USA with title *A James Stephens Reader*. New York: Macmillan, 1962.

Strong, Eithne. *Songs of Living*. Pref. Dublin: Ptd. at the Dolmen for the Runa Press, 1961.

Swift, Jonathan. *Gulliver's Travels*. Ed. with an intro. New York: Macmillan, 1917. London: Harrap, 1919.

——. *Poems of Jonathan Swift*. Sel. with an intro. New York: Collier, 1962.

Treasury of Irish Folklore: Stories, traditions, legends, humor, wisdom, ballads, and songs of the Irish people. Ed. with an intro. New York: Crown, 1954. Rev. ed., 1962. 2nd rev. ed., 1967.

Ussher, Arland, and Carl von Metzradt. *Enter These Enchanted Woods.* Pref. Dublin: Dolmen, 1967.

BIOGRAPHICAL AND CRITICAL

Bowen, Zack. *Padraic Colum.* Carbondale: Southern Illinois University, 1971.

Daniel Corkery (1878-1964)

POEMS, PLAYS, FICTION

An Doras Dunta. Baile Átha Cliath: Oifig an tSalthair, 1953.

I bhreasail: A book of lyrics. London: Mathews; Dublin: Talbot, 1921.

Earth Out of Earth. Dublin and Cork: Talbot, 1939.

The Hounds of Banba. Dublin: Talbot; London: Unwin, 1920. New York: Heubsch; New York: Viking, 1922.

The Labour Leader: A play in three acts. Dublin: Talbot; London: Unwin, 1920.

A Munster Twilight. Dublin: Talbot, 1916. London: Unwin; New York: Stokes, 1917.

A Munster Twilight and The Hounds of Banba. Dublin: Talbot [1925].

Resurrection: A play in one act. Dublin: Talbot [1942].

The Stormy Hills. Dublin: Talbot; London: Cape, 1929.

The Threshold of Quiet. Prologue. Dublin: Talbot; London: Unwin, 1917. New York: Stokes, 1921.

The Wager; and other stories. New York: Devin-Adair, 1950.

The Yellow Bittern; and other plays. Dublin: Talbot; London: Unwin. 1920.

CRITICAL WRITINGS

Farming in the Irish Free State. London: Empire Marketing Board, 1930.

The Fortunes of the Irish Language. Dublin: Pub. for the Cultural Relations Committee on Ireland by J. C. Fallon, 1954.

The Hidden Ireland: A story of Gaelic Munster in the eighteenth century. Dublin: Gill, 1923.

The Philosophy of the Gaelic League. Átha Cliath: Connradh na Gaedhilge: Powell, 1948.

Synge and Anglo-Irish Literature: A Study. Dublin and Cork: Cork University Press with the Educational Co. of Ireland; New York: Longmans, Green, 1931.

What's This About the Gaelic League. Baile Átha Cliath: Connradh na Gaedhilge [1942].

JOINT AUTHOR

With Seamas Ó hAodha. *An Clochar, Drama um mhiorbhuilt.* Átha Cliath: Cló-lucht an Thalbotaig [1919].

FOREWORDS BY

Chavasse, Moirin. *Terrence MacSwinney.* Dublin: Clonmore and Reynolds; London: Burns and Oates, 1961.

MacDonagh, Thomas. *Literature in Ireland: Studies in Irish and Anglo-Irish.* Intro. Dublin: Talbot; London: Unwin, 1939. The 1916 ed. did not have Corkery's intro.

BIOGRAPHY AND CRITICISM

Saul, G. B. *Daniel Corkery.* (Irish Writers Series). Lewisburg, Pa.: Bucknell University Press [n. d.]

Cecil Day Lewis (1904-   )

BIBLIOGRAPHY

Handley-Taylor, Geoffery and Smith, Timothy D'Arch. *C. Day Lewis. The Poet Laureate.* A bibliography. Introduced by W. H. Auden.

Chicago and London: St. James Press, 1968. General and limited edition of 100 numbered copies signed by The Poet Laureate.

COLLECTED AND SELECTED POEMS

C. Day Lewis. *Selections from His Poetry*. Sel. with an intro. and notes by Patrick Dickinson. London: Chatto and Windus, 1967.

Cecil Day Lewis. Selected Poems. London: Eyre and Spottiswoode [1943].

Collected Poems, 1929-1933: Transitional Poem, From Feathers to Iron, The Magnetic Mountain. London: Hogarth, 1935. Same with A Hope for Poetry. New York: Random House, 1935.

Collected Poems, 1929-1936. Fore. London: Hogarth, 1948.

Collected Poems of C. Day Lewis. London: Cape with the Hogarth Press, 1954.

Poems, 1943-1947. London: Cape; New York: Oxford, 1948.

Selected Poems. London: Hogarth, 1940.

Selected Poems. Harmondsworth: Penguin, 1951. Rev. ed. 1957.

Selected Poems. New York: Harper & Row, 1967.

INDIVIDUAL TITLES

POETRY

Beechen Vigil; and other poems. London: Fortune, 1925.

Christmas Eve. London: Faber and Faber, 1954.

Country Comets. London: Hopkinson, 1928.

From Feathers to Iron. London: Hogarth, 1931.

The Gate; and other poems. London: Cape, 1962.

An Italian Visit: Poems. London: Cape; New York: Harper, 1953.

The Magnetic Mountain: Poems. London: Hogarth, 1933. Reg. and limited edition of 100 numbered copies signed by the author.

Noah and the Waters. London: Hogarth, 1936. 100 copies. See also *A Time to Dance*.

Overtures to Death; and other poems. London: Cape, 1938.

Pegasus; and other poems. London: Cape, 1957. Same with "The Meeting." New York: Harper, 1958.

Poems in Wartime. London: Cape, 1940.

Requiem for the Living. New York and Evanston: Harper, 1964.

The Room; and other poems. London: Cape, 1965.

Short Is the Time: Poems, 1936-1943. New York: Oxford, 1945. Pub. in England as *Overtures to Death* [1938] and *Word Over All* [1943].

A Time to Dance; and other poems. London: Hogarth, 1935. Same with title *Noah and the Waters; and other poems with an essay, Revolution in Writing.* New York: Random House, 1936. Reg. and limited edition of 100 numbered copies, signed by the author.

Transitional Poem. London: Hogarth, 1929.

The Whispering Roots; and other poems. New York: Harper & Row, 1970.

Word Over All: Poems. London: Cape, 1943.

FICTION

Child of Misfortune: A novel. London: Cape, 1939.

Dick Willoughby. Oxford: Blackwell [1933]. New York: Random House, 1938.

The Friendly Tree: A novel. London: Cape, 1936. New York and London: Harper [1937].

The Otterbury Incident: A tale. London: Putnam, 1948. New York: Viking, 1949.

Starting Point: A novel. London: Cape, 1937. New York and London: Harper, 1938.

CRITICISM BY

The Colloquial Element in English Poetry. The Robert Spence Watson Memorial Lecture for 1947 delivered before The Literary and Philosophic Society of Newcastle Upon Tyne, March 24th, 1947. Newcastle Upon Tyne: Pub. by The Literary and Philosophic Society of Newcastle Upon Tyne, 1947.

Enjoying Poetry: A reader's guide. London: Pub. at the Cambridge University Press for the National Book League, 1947. Rev. ed., 1956.

The Grand Manner [Nottingham]: University of Nottingham [1952].

A Hope for Poetry. Oxford: Blackwell, 1934. Rpd. with a postscript. Oxford: Blackwell, 1936.

The Lyrical Poetry of Thomas Hardy. From the Proceedings of the British Academy, Vol. XXXVII. London: Amen House [1953].

The Lyric Impulse. The Charles Eliot Norton Lectures, 1964-1965. Fore. Cambridge: Harvard University, 1965.

*A Need for Poetry? Hull: University of Hull, 1968.

Notable Images of Virtue: Emily Bronte, George Meredith, W. B. Yeats. Being the sixth series of lectures on the Chancellor Dunning Trust. Lectures delivered at Queen's University, Kingston, Ontario, 1954. Toronto: Ryerson, 1954.

On Translating Poetry. Abington-on-Thames: Abbey Press, 1970.

The Poetic Image. The Clark Lecture Given at Cambridge in 1946. London: Cape; New York: Oxford, 1947.

Poetry for You: A book for boys and girls on the enjoyment of poetry. Oxford: Blackwell, 1944. New York: Oxford, 1947.

The Poet's Task. An inaugural lecture delivered before the University of Oxford on 1 June 1951. Oxford: Clarendon, 1951.

The Poet's Way to Knowledge. Cambridge: Cambridge University, 1957.

Revolution in Writing. London: Hogarth, 1935.

We're Not Going To Do Nothing. (A reply to Mr. Aldous Huxley's pamphlet, "What Are You Going To Do About It?"). London: Left Review, 1936. Reg. and ltd. ed. of 50 numbered copies signed by the author.

AUTOBIOGRAPHY

The Buried Day. London: Chatto and Windus; New York: Harper, 1960.

UNDER THE PSEUDONYM OF NICHOLAS BLAKE

The Beast Must Die. London: Pub. for the Crime Club by Collins; New York and London: Harper, 1938.

The Case of the Abominable Snowman. London: Pub. for the Crime Club by Collins, 1941. Pub. in the USA with title *The Corpse in the Snowman*. New York and London: Harper, 1941.

The Deadly Joker. London: Pub. for the Crime Club by Collins, 1963.

The Dreadful Hollow. London: Pub. for the Crime Club by Collins; New York: Harper, 1953.

End of the Chapter. London: Pub. for the Crime Club by Collins; New York: Harper, 1957.

Head of a Traveler. London: Pub. for the Crime Club by Collins, 1940. Pub. in the USA with title *The Summer Camp Mystery*. New York and London: Harper, 1940. Same with title *Malice with Murder*. New York: Pyramid, 1964.

Minute for Murder. London: Pub. for the Crime Club by Collins; New York and London: Harper, 1947.

The Morning after Death. New York: Harper, 1966.

The Nicholas Blake Omnibus. Intro. London: Collins, 1966.

A Penknife in My Heart. London: Pub. for the Crime Club by Collins; New York and London: Harper, 1935.

The Private Wound. London: Pub. for the Crime Club by Collins; New York: Harper, 1968.

A Question of Proof. London: Pub. for the Crime Club by Collins; New York and London: Harper, 1935.

The Sad Variety. London and Glasgow: Collins; New York and Evanston: Harper, 1964.

The Smiler with the Knife. London: Pub. for the Crime Club by Collins; New York and London: Harper, 1939.

A Tangled Web. London: Collins; New York: Harper, 1956.

There's Trouble Brewing. London: Pub. for the Crime Club by Collins; New York and London: Harper, 1937.

Thou Shell of Death: A novel. London: Pub. for the Crime Club by Collins; 1936. Pub. in the USA with title *Shell of Death*. New York and London: Harper, 1936.

The Whisper in the Gloom. London: Pub. for the Crime Club by Collins; New York and London: Harper, 1954.

The Widow's Curse. New York: Harper, 1959.

The Worm of Death. London and Glasgow: Collins; New York: Harper, 1961.

JOINT AUTHOR

With Susan Stebbling. *Imagination and Thinking. Two Addresses.* London: British Institute of Adult Education, 1936.

EDITED BY

With W. H. Auden. *Oxford Poetry.* Oxford: Blackwell, 1927.

Blunden, Edmund Charles. *The Midnight Skaters: Poems for young readers.* Chosen with an intro. by Day Lewis. London: Bodley Head, 1968.

Browning, Robert. *The Poems of Robert Browning.* New York: Heritage, 1971.

A Book of English Lyrics. London: Chatto and Windus, 1961. Pub. in the USA with title *English Lyric Poems, 1500-1900.* New York: Appleton-Century-Crofts, 1961.

The Echoing Green. An Anthology of Verse. 3 vols. Oxford: Blackwell, 1937, 1941, 1942.

With Charles Fenby. *Anatomy of Oxford.* London: Cape, 1938.

Keats, John. *A Choice of Keats' Verse.* Selected with Intro. London: Faber and Faber, 1971.

With John Lehmann and T. A. Jackson. *Ralph Fox: A Writer in Arms.* Intro. London: Lawrence-Wishort, 1937.

With John Lehmann. *The Chatto Book of Modern Poetry, 1915-1955.* Intro. London: Chatto and Windus, 1956.

Meredith, George. *Modern Love.* Intro. London: Hart-Davis, 1948.

The Mind in Chains: Socialism and the Cultural revolution. London: Muller, 1937.

Owen, Wilfred. *Collected Poems of Wilfred Owen.* Intro. and Notes. Memoir by Edmund Blunden. London: Chatto and Windus, 1963. New York: New Directions: c1963, 1964.

Palgrave, Francis Turner. *The Golden Treasury of the best songs and lyrical poems in the English Language.* Intro. and additional poems, sel. and arr. London and Glasgow: Collins, 1954.

Ricketts, Charles S. *Self-portrait: Taken from the Letters and Journals of Charles Ricketts*, R.A. Coll. and comp. by T. Sturge Moore. London: Davies, 1939.

With D. Kilham Roberts, Edwin Muir, and Rosamond Lehmann. *Orion: A miscellany.* 4 vols. London: Nicholson and Watson, 1945-46. Muir was ed. only for Vol. II. Roberts was only ed. of Vol. IV.

With L. A. G. Strong. *A New Anthology of Modern Verse, 1920-1940.* Intro. London: Methuen, 1941.

TRANSLATED BY

Gazdag, Erzsi. *The Tomtit in the Rain.* London: Chatto and Windus, 1971.

Valéry, Paul. *The Graveyard by the Sea. Le Cimetière Marin.* London: Secker and Warburg, 1945. French and English.

Virgil. *The Aeneid.* London: Hogarth; New York: Oxford University, 1952. Reg. and limited edition of 150 numbered and signed copies.

——. *The Eclogues and Georgics of Virgil.* London: Cape, 1963. Garden City, N.Y.: Anchor, 1964.

——. *The Georgics of Virgil.* London: Cape, 1940. Same with intro. by Louis Bromfield. New York: Oxford University, 1947.

CRITICAL STUDIES ABOUT

Dyment, Clifford. *C. Day Lewis.* London, New York, and Toronto: Pub. by Longmans, Green for the British Council and The National Book League, 1955. Writers and Their Work, No. 62.

Denis Devlin (1908-1958)

POEMS

Collected Poems. Ed. with intro. by Brian Coffey. Dublin: Dolmen, 1964. First pub. as a special number of *The University Review* in 1963.

The Heavenly Foreigner. Ed. with intro. and notes by Brian Coffey. Dublin: Dolmen, 1967. 750 copies.

Intercessions: Poems. London: Europa, 1937. 300 numbered copies with 1-25 signed.

Lough Derg; and other poems. New York: Reynal and Hitchcock, 1946.

Selected Poems. Ed. with pref. by Allan Tate and Robert Penn Warren. New York: Holt, Rinehart, and Winston, 1963.

JOINT AUTHOR

With Brian Coffey. *Poems*. Dublin: Pub. for the authors by Thom, 1930.

TRANSLATED BY

Leger, Alexis Saint-Leger (St. John Perse). *Exile; and other poems*. Trans. Devlin and others. New York: Pantheon, 1949.

――――. *Rains (Pluies)*. The French poem with an English trans. by Denis Devlin. Sewanee, Tennessee: *The Sewanee Review*, 1945. French and English. Rpd. from the October 1944 issue of *The Sewanee Review*.

――――. *Snows (Neiges)*. The French poem with an English translation by Denis Devlin. Sewanee, Tennessee: *The Sewanee Review*, 1945. French and English. Rpd. from the April 1944 issue of *The Sewanee Review*.

Valery, Paul. *Selected Writings*. Translated by Denis Devlin and others. New York: New Directions, 1964.

Edward Morton Drax Plunkett, Lord Dunsany (1878-1957)

COLLECTED PLAYS

Alexander; and three small plays. London and New York: Putnam, 1925. New York: Putnam, 1926. In 1925 separate issue of each play: *Alexander, The Amusements of Khan Kharudu, The Evil Kettle, The Old King's Tale*.

Five Plays. London: Richards; London and New York: Putnam; New York: Kennerley, 1914. Putnam issued each play separately also: *The Gods of the Mountain, The Golden Doom, King Argimenes and The Unknown Warrior, The Glittering Gate, The Lost Silk Hat*.

Plays for Earth and Air. London and Toronto: Heinemann, 1937.

Plays of Gods and Men. Pref. Dublin: Talbot; London: Unwin; New York: Putnam; Boston: Luce, 1917. Separate issue by Talbot also: *The Laughter of the Gods, The Queen's Enemies, The Tents of the Arabs, A Night at an Inn.*

Plays of Near and Far. London and New York: Putnam, 1922. 500 copies.

Seven Modern Comedies. London and New York: Putnam, 1928. New York: Putnam, 1929. Separate issue in 1928 also: *Atalanta in Wimbledon, The Raffle, The Journey of the Soul, In Holy Russia, His Sainted Grandmother, The Hopeless Passion of Mr. Bunyan, The Jest of Hahalaba.*

COLLECTED FICTION

The Book of Wonder: A chronicle of little adventures at the edge of the world. London: Heinemann, 1912. Boston: Luce, 1913.

A Dreamer's Tales. London: Allen, 1910. Boston: Luce [1916]. Same with title *A Dreamer's Tales; and other stories.* Intro. by Padraic Colum. New York: Boni and Liveright, 1919.

Fifty-one Tales. London: Mathews; New York: Kennerley, 1915.

The Fourth Book of Jorkens. London: Jarrolds [1948]. Sauk City, Wis.: Arkham, 1948.

Jorkens Remembers Africa. New York and Toronto: Longmans, Green, 1934. Same with title *Mr. Jorkens Remembers Africa.* Pref. London and Toronto: Heinemann, 1934.

The Last Book of Wonder. Boston: Luce, 1916.

The Little Tales of Smethers; and other stories. London: Jarrolds, 1952.

The Man Who Ate the Phoenix. London: Jarrolds [1949].

Mr. Jorkens Remembers Africa. See *Jorkens Remembers Africa.*

The Sword of Welleran; and other stories. London: Allen, 1908. Boston: Luce [1916]. Same with title *The Sword of Welleran; and other tales of enchantment.* New York: Devin-Adair, 1954.

Tales of Three Hemispheres. Boston: Luce, 1919. London: Unwin, 1920.

Tales of War. Dublin: Talbot; London: Unwin; Boston: Little, Brown, 1918.

Tales of Wonder. London: Mathews, 1916.

The Travel Tales of Mr. Joseph Jorkens. London and New York: Putnam, 1931.

SELECTED WORKS

Gods, Men and Ghosts: The best supernatural fiction of Lord Dunsany. Selected with an intro. by E. F. Bleiler. New York: Dover, 1972.

Selections from the writings of Lord Dunsany. Intro. by W. B. Yeats. Dundrum: Cuala, 1912. 250 copies.

Wandering Songs: A collection of original poems together with trans. from Turkish poetry. London, New York, and Melbourne: Hutchinson [1943].

INDIVIDUAL PLAYS

Alexander: A play in four acts. See *Alexander; and three small plays.*

The Amusements of Khan Kharudu. See *Alexander; and three small plays.*

Atalanta in Wimbledon. See *Seven Modern Comedies.*

Cheezo: A Comedy in one act. London and New York: Putnam, n.d.

The Compromise of the King and the Golden Isles. New York: Designed and ptd. for the Grolier Club by T. M. Cleland, 1924. 300 numbered copies. London and New York: Putnam, n.d.

The Evil Kettle. See *Alexander; and three small plays.*

Fame and the Poet. London and New York: Putnam [192?].

Flight of the Queen. London: Putnam, n.d.

The Glittering Gate. See *Five Plays.*

The Gods of the Mountain. London and New York: Putnam, 1914. See *Five Plays.*

The Golden Doom: A one-act play. London: Putnam, 1913. See *Five Plays.*

Good Bargain: A play. London: Putnam, n.d.

His Sainted Grandmother: A play. See *Seven Modern Comedies.*

The Hopeless Passion of Mr. Bunyan: A play. See *Seven Modern Comedies.*

If: A play in four acts. London and New York: Putnam, 1921. New York: Putnam, 1922.

If Shakespeare Lived To-Day: A play. London: Putnam, n.d.

In Holy Russia: A play. See *Seven Modern Comedies.*

The Jest of Hahalaba: A play. See *Seven Modern Comedies.*

The Journey of the Soul: A play. See *Seven Modern Comedies.*

King Argimenes and the Unknown Warrior. See *Five Plays.*

The Laughter of the Gods. See *Plays of Gods and Men.*

Lord Adrian: A play in three acts. Waltham, St. Lawrence: Golden Cockerel, 1933. 325 numbered copies.

The Lost Silk Hat. See *Five Plays.*

Mr. Faithful: A comedy in three acts. Los Angeles, London, and New York: French, 1935.

A Night at an Inn: A play in one act. New York: Sunwise Turn, 1916. London: Putnam, 1922. New ed. New York: Sunwise Turn, 1925.

The Old Folk of the Centuries: A play. London: Mathews and Marot [1930]. 900 numbered copies: 1-100 signed, 101-850 for sale, 851-900 hors-commerce.

The Old King's Tale. See *Alexander; and three small plays.*

The Queen's Enemies: A play. New York: French, 1916. London: Putnam, 1922.

The Raffle: A play. See *Seven Modern Comedies.*

The Tents of the Arabs: A play. See *Plays of Gods and Men.*

FICTION

Blessings of Pan. London and New York: Putnam, 1927.

Carcassonne. Boston: Ptd. by Luce for Miss Virginia Berry [1916].

The Chronicles of Rodriguez. London and New York: Putnam, 1922. 500 numbered copies signed by Dunsany and Sime (illustrator). Pub. in the USA with title *Don Rodriguez.* New York and London: Putnam, 1922.

The Curse of the Wise Woman. London: Heinemann; New York and Toronto: Longmans, Green, 1933.

Don Rodriguez. See *The Chronicles of Rodriguez.*

The Gods of Pegana. London: Mathews, 1905. Boston: Luce, 1916.

Guerilla: A novel. London and Toronto: Heinemann; New York and Indianapolis: Bobbs-Merrill, 1944.

His Fellow Man: A novel. London: Jarrolds, 1952.

If I Were Dictator: The pronouncements of the Grand Macaroni. London: Methuen, 1934.

Jorkens Borrows Another Whiskey. London: Jarrolds, 1954.

Jorkens Has a Large Whiskey. London: Putnam, 1940.

The King of Elfland's Daughter. Pref. London and New York: Putnam, 1924. 250 numbered copies signed by Dunsany and Sime (illustrator) and unlimited ed.

The Last Revolution. London: Jarrolds, 1951.

Rory and Bran. London and Toronto: Heinemann, 1936. New York: Putnam, 1937.

The Story of Mona Sheehy. London and Toronto: Heinemann, 1939. New York: Harper, 1940.

The Strange Journeys of Colonel Polders. London: Jarrolds, 1950.

Time and the Gods. London: Heinemann, 1906. Boston: Luce [1913]. Same with a new pref. London and New York: Putnam, 1923. 250 numbered copies signed by Dunsany and Sime (illustrator).

Up in the Hills: A tale. London and Toronto: Heinemann, 1935. London and New York: Putnam, 1936.

Why the Milkman Shudders When He Perceives the Dawn. Fostoria, Ohio: Pvt. Ptd. 1925.

POEMS

Fifty Poems. London and New York: Putnam, 1929.

A Journey: A poem. London: Macdonald [1943]. 250 numbered and initialed copies.

Mirage Water: Poems. London: Putnam, 1938. Philadelphia: Contemporary Poets, 1939.

To Awaken Pegasus; and other poems. Oxford: Ronald, 1949.

War Poems. London and Melbourne: Hutchinson [1941].

The Year: A poem. London, Melbourne, Sydney, and New York: Jarrolds, 1946.

NON-FICTION

Building a Sentence. Fore. by Lawton Mackall. New York: Marchbanks, n.d.

The Donnellan Lectures, 1943. Delivered at Trinity College, Dublin, on March 2nd, 3rd, 4th. London and Toronto: Heinemann, 1945.

A Glimpse from a Watch Tower. A series of brilliant and challenging essays on man's outlook in an uncertain future, written between July 7th and August 21st, 1945. London: Jarrolds, 1946.

My Ireland. London: Jarrolds; New York and London: Funk; Toronto: Oxford, 1937. Rev. ed., London: Jarrolds, 1950.

My Talks with Dean Spanley. London: Heinemann; New York: Putnam, 1936.

Nowadays: An essay. Boston: Four Seas, 1918. 500 copies on Venetian handmade paper and unlimited ed.

Patches of Sunlight: An autobiography. London and Toronto: Heinemann; New York: Reynal and Hitchcock, 1938.

The Sirens Wake: Autobiographical reminiscences. London: Jarrolds, 1945.

Unhappy Far-off Things. London: Mathews; Boston: Little, Brown, 1919.

While the Sirens Slept: Autobiographical reminiscences. London, Melbourne, and New York: Jarrolds [1944].

TRANSLATED BY

With Michael Oakley. *The Collected Works of Horace.* Intro. by Oakley. New York: Dutton, 1960. London: Dent, 1961.

The Odes of Horace. London and Toronto: Heinemann. 1947.

INTRODUCTION

Caldwell, Thomas (ed.) *The Golden Book of Modern English Poetry, 1870-1920.* London and Toronto: Dent, 1922. Same with added poems and title *The Golden Book of Modern English Poetry, 1870-1930* in 1930.

Coblentz, Stanton A. *Time's Travellers.* Mill Valley, Calif.: Wings, 1952.

Crone, Annie. *Bridie Steen.* London: Heinemann, 1949.

Hamilton, Mary. *Green and Gold.* London: Wingate, 1948.

Ireland, L'Irlande, Irland: A book of photographs. London: Anglo-Italian [1959]. English, French, German.

Lavin, Mary. *Tales from Bective Bridge.* London: Joseph, 1943.

Ledwidge, Francis. *The Complete Poems of Francis Ledwidge.* London: Jenkins; New York: Brentano's, 1919.

————. *Last Songs.* London: Jenkins, 1918.

————. *Songs of the Fields.* London: Jenkins, 1916.

————. *Songs of Peace.* London: Jenkins, 1917.

MacCall, Seamas. *Gods in Motley.* London: Constable, 1935.

Machen, Arthur. *A Hill of Dreams.* London: Richards, 1954.

Meredith, George. *The Egoist.* London: Oxford University, 1947.

*Price, Nancy. *Acquainted with the Night: A book of dreams.* Oxford: Ronald, 1952.

*Lady Wentworth. *Drift of the Storm.* Oxford: Ronald, 1951.

CRITICAL AND BIOGRAPHICAL STUDIES

Amory, Mark. *Lord Dunsany: A biography.* London: Collins, 1972.

Bierstadt, Edward H. *Dunsany the Dramatist.* Boston: Little, Brown, 1917. New and revised ed. Boston: Little, Brown, 1919.

Bowen, Zack. *Lord Edward Dunsany.* (Irish Writers Series) Lewisburg, Pa.: Bucknell University [n. d.].

Rattray, R. F. *Poets in the Flesh: Tagore, Yeats, Dunsany, Stephens, Drinkwater.* Cambridge: Golden Head, 1961.

Smith, Hazel Littlefield. *Lord Dunsany: King of dreams. A personal portrait.* Foreword by Stanton Coblentz. New York: Exposition, 1959.

Lawrence Durrell (1912-   )

STANDARD BIBLIOGRAPHY

Potter, Robert A., and Brooke Whiting. *Lawrence Durrell: A Checklist.* Los Angeles: Library of the University of California at Los Angeles, 1961.

PROSE

The Alexandria Quartet: Justine, Baltazar, Mount Olive, Clea. Rev. ed. London: Faber and Faber, 1962.

Beccafico. Le Becfique. Trans. and ed. F. J. Temple. Montpellier: La Licorne, 1963. 153 signed and numbered copies. English and French.

The Blue Thirst. Two lectures. Santa Barbara: Capra, 1975. Regular and signed ltd. ed. 200 copies.

Brassaï. New York: Museum of Modern Art, 1968.

La Descente du Styx. Down the Styx. Trans. F. J. Temple. Montpellier: La Licorne, 1964. 250 signed and numbered copies. French and English.

Down the Styx. Preface by F. J. Temple. Santa Barbara, Calif.: Capricorn, 1971. 200 hardbound copies, numbered and signed; 800 softbound copies.

Monsieur: A Novel. London: Faber and Faber, 1974. New York: Viking, 1975.

Nunquam: A Novel. London: Faber and Faber; New York: Dutton, 1970.

The Plant-Magic Man. Santa Barbara, Calif.: Capra, 1973.

Sauve qui peut. Nicholas Bentley drew the pictures. London: Faber and Faber, 1966. New York: Dutton, c1966, 1967.

Spirit of Place: Letters and Essays on Travel. Edited by Alan G. Thomas. London: Faber and Faber; New York: Dutton, 1969.

Tunc: A Novel. London: Faber and Faber; New York: Dutton, 1968.

POETRY

Collected Poems. New and rev. ed. London: Faber and Faber, 1968.

*Faustus. A poem. n. p. 19——. Ed. limited to 50 copies.

The Ikons; and other poems. London: Faber and Faber, 1966. New York: Dutton, 1967.

In Arcadia. London: Turret Books, 1968. With the same title. Music by Wallace Southam. With music. London: Trigram, 1968. 100 copies.

On the Suchness of the Old Boy. Drawings by Sappho Durrell. London: Turret Books, 1972. Limited edition of 226 copies, 26 lettered and not for sale; 200 are numbered and signed by poet and artist.

The Red Limbo Lingo: A poetry notebook. London: Faber and Faber; New York: Dutton, 1971.

Selected Poems, 1935-1963. London: Faber and Faber, 1964.

Vega and Other Poems. London: Faber and Faber; Woodstock, N.Y.: Overlook, 1973.

PLAYS

Acte: A play. London: Faber and Faber, 1965. New York: Dutton, c. 1965, 1966.

An Irish Faustus: A morality of nine scenes. London: Faber and Faber, 1963. New York: Dutton, 1964.

Ulysses Come Back. "An outline-sketch of a musical based upon the last three love-affairs of Ulysses the Greek adventurer of mythology, adapted rather light-heartedly from Homer." London: Turret Books, c. 1970. "99 copies only issued (including 2-12″ 33⅓ rpm phonodiscs) in June 1970, numbered and signed by author."

LETTERS

Lawrence Durrell. Henry Miller. *A Private Correspondence.* Ed. with an intro. by George Wickes. London: Faber and Faber; New York: Dutton, 1963.

JOINT AUTHOR

Lawrence Durrell, Elizabeth Jennings, R. S. Thomas. *Penguin Modern Poets*, No. 1. Harmondsworth: Penguin, 1962.

PREFACE BY

An Introduction to the Fifth Antiquarian Book Fair Handlist of Exhibitors. London: National Book League, 1962.

*Armstrong, Terence Ian Fytton. *Some Poems.* Intro. by Lawrence Durrell. n.p. 1971.

Groddeck, Georg W. *The Book of the It.* Intro. by Lawrence Durrell. Trans. from German by V. M. E. Collins. London: Vision, 1949.

Lear, Edward. *Lear's Corfu: An anthology drawn from the painter's letters.* Corfu: Corfu Travel, c.1965.

EDITED BY

Wordsworth, William. *Wordsworth.* (Penguin Poets Series). Edited by
Lawrence Durrell. Harmondsworth: Penguin, 1973.

TRANSLATED BY

Bosquet, Alain. *Selected Poems.* Trans. from French by Wallace Fowlie,
Lawrence Durrell, Samuel Beckett, Jean and Elisabeth Malaquais.
Athens, Ohio: Ohio University, 1973.

BIOGRAPHICAL AND CRITICAL STUDIES ABOUT

Durrell, Lawrence. *The Big Supposer: A dialogue with Marc Alyn.* Illus.
with paintings by Lawrence Durrell. Trans. from French by Fran-
cine Barker. (French copyright 1972, Pierre Belfond, Paris. Translation copyright, 1973, Albelard-Schuman, London.) New York:
Grove, 1974.

Fraser, G. S. *Lawrence Durrell: A Study.* London: Faber and Faber,
1968. With title *Lawrence Durrell: A Critical Study.* New York:
Dutton, 1968.

Friedman, Alan Warren. *Lawrence Durrell and the Alexandria Quartet:
Art for Love's Sake.* Norman, Okla.: University of Oklahoma,
1970.

Moore, Harry T., ed. *The World of Lawrence Durrell.* Carbondale,
Ill.: Southern Illinois University, 1962.

Perles, Alfred. *My Friend Lawrence Durrell: An intimate memoir on the
author of the Alexandria Quartet.* With portraits. Northwood, England: Scorpion, 1961.

Unterecker, John. *Lawrence Durrell.* New York: Columbia University,
1964.

Weigel, John A. *Lawrence Durrell.* New York: Twayne, 1965.

John St. John Greer Ervine (1883-1971)

COLLECTED AND SELECTED WORKS

Eight O'Clock; and other studies. Dublin: Maunsel, 1913.

Four Irish Plays. New York: Macmillan [1911]. London: Maunsel, 1914.

Four One-Act Plays. London: Allen and Unwin; New York: Macmillan, 1928. Also issued separately by Allen and Unwin: *The Magnanimous Lover, Progress, Ole George Comes to Tea, She Was No Lady.*

The Mountain; and other stories. London: Allen and Unwin; New York: Macmillan, 1928.

Old Mrs. Clifford and Safety. London: Polybooks [1944].

The St. John Greer Omnibus. London: Collins [1933].

PLAYS

Anthony and Anna: A comedy in three acts. London: Allen and Unwin; New York: Macmillan, 1925. Rev. ed. in 1936.

Boyd's Shop: A comedy in four acts. London: Allen and Unwin; New York: Macmillan, 1936.

The First Mrs. Frazer: A comedy in three acts. London: Chatto and Windus, 1929.

Friends and Relations: A comedy in three acts. London: Allen and Unwin, 1947.

Jane Clegg: A play in three acts. London: Sidgwick and Jackson, 1914. New York: Holt, c1914, 1915.

John Ferguson: A play in four acts. Dublin and London: Maunsel; London: Allen and Unwin; New York: Macmillan, 1915. Same with intro. by Ervine. New York: Macmillan, 1920. London: Allen and Unwin, 1934.

The Lady of Belmont: A play in five acts. London: Allen and Unwin [1923]. New York: Macmillan, 1924.

The Magnanimous Lover: A play in one act. Dublin and London: Maunsel, 1912. See *Four One-Act Plays.*

Mary, Mary, Quite Contrary: A light comedy in four acts. London: Allen and Unwin; New York: Macmillan, 1923.

Mixed Marriage: A play in four acts. Dublin: Maunsel, 1911. London: Allen and Unwin, 1920.

My Brother Tom: A country comedy in three acts. London: Allen and Unwin, 1952.

Morals for Amateurs. New York: French, 1930.

Ole George Comes to Tea. See *Four One-Act Plays*.

People of Our Class: A comedy in three acts. London: Allen and Unwin: New York: Macmillan, 1936.

Private Enterprise: A play in three acts. London: Allen and Unwin, 1948.

Progress. London: Allen and Unwin, 1931.

Robert's Wife: A comedy in three acts. London: Allen and Unwin; New York: Macmillan, 1938.

Sauce for the Goose. London: Allen and Unwin, n.d.

She Was No Lady. See *Four One-Act Plays*.

The Ship: A play in three acts. London: Allen and Unwin; New York: Macmillan, 1922.

FICTION

Alice and a Family: A story of South London. London and Dublin: Maunsel; New York: Macmillan, 1915.

Changing Winds: A novel. Dublin and London: Maunsel; New York: Macmillan, 1917.

The Christies. London: Allen and Unwin, 1949.

The First Mrs. French: A novel. London: Collins; New York: Macmillan, 1931.

The Foolish Lovers. London: Collins; New York: Macmillan, 1920.

Mrs. Martin's Man. Dublin and London: Maunsel, 1914. New York: Macmillan, 1915.

Sophia. London and New York: Macmillan, 1941.

The Wayward Man. London: Collins; New York: Macmillan, 1927.

NON-FICTION

The Alleged Art of the Cinema. University of London. University College Union Society. Foundation Week Oration, 1934. Shrewsbury: Wilding, 1934.

Bernard Shaw: His life, work, and friends. London: Constable; New York: Morrow, 1956.

Craigavon, Ulsterman. London: Allen and Unwin, 1949.

Francis Place: The Tailor of Charing Cross. London: The Fabian Society, October, 1912.

The Future of the Press. London: World's Press News [1933].

God's Soldier: General William Booth. 2 vols. London and Toronto: Heinemann, 1934. New York: Macmillan, 1935.

How to Write a Play. London: Allen and Unwin; New York: Macmillan, 1928.

If I Were Dictator. London: Methuen, 1934.

Is Liberty Lost? London: Individualist Bookshop, 1941.

A Journey to Jerusalem. London: Hamilton, 1936. New York: Macmillan, 1937.

The Organized Theatre: A plea for civics. London: Allen and Unwin; New York: Macmillan, 1924.

Oscar Wilde: A present time appraisal. London: Allen and Unwin; New York: Macmillan [1951].

Parnell. London: Benn; Boston: Little, Brown, 1925.

Sir Edward Carson and the Ulster Movement. Dublin and London: Maunsel, 1915. New York: Dodd, Mead, 1916.

Some Impressions of My Elders. New York: Macmillan, 1922. London: Allen and Unwin, 1923.

The State and the Soul. The Essex Hall Lecture, 1939. London: Lindsey [1939].

The Theatre in My Time. London: Rich and Cowan, 1933. New York: Mussey, 1934.

Ulster. Belfast: Ulster Tourist Development Association, 1926.

INTRODUCTION BY

George W. Harris. Fore. by St. John Ervine. A biographical note, George Harris in the theatre, by Basil Dean. G. W. H. by Lascelles Abercrombie. The Function of the Scenic Designer by George W. Harris. London: Nisbet, 1930. 425 numbered copies.

Irwin, Florence. *The Cookin' Woman: Irish country recipes and others.* Intro. Edinburgh: Oliver and Boyd, 1949.

Pogson, Rex. *Miss Horniman and the Gaiety Theatre, Manchester.* Fore. London: Rockliff, 1952.

Quinn, Hugh. *Mrs. McConaghy's Money: A Quiet Twelfth. Collecting the Rent.* Intro. London: Constable, 1932.

Shakespeare, William. *Complete Works of William Shakespeare.* Intro. by Ervine and Sir Henry Irving. London and Glasgow: Collins [1937].

————. *The Tragedy of King Richard II.* Ed. with an intro. London: Macmillan, 1935.

————. *King Richard II.* Ed. by Lionel Aldred with an intro. by St. John Ervine. Notes. London: Macmillan, 1935.

George Fitzmaurice (1877-1963)

PLAYS

The Country Dressmaker: A play in three acts. Dublin and London: Maunsel, 1914.

Five Plays. Dublin and London: Maunsel, 1914.

Plays. Ed. with an intro. by Austin Clarke. Vol. 1. *Dramatic Fantasies.* Dublin: Dolmen; London: Oxford University; Chester Springs, Pa.: Dufour, 1967. Vol. 2. *Folk Plays.* Vol. 3. *Realistic Plays.* Ed. with introductions by H. K. Slaughter. Dublin: Dolmen; London: Oxford University; Chester Springs, Pa.: Dufour, 1970.

The Crows of Mephistopheles and Other Stories. Ed. with an intro. by Robert Hogan. Dublin: Dolmen, 1970.

BIOGRAPHY AND CRITICISM

McGuiness, Arthur E. *George Fitzmaurice.* (Irish Writers Series). Lewisburg, Pa.: Bucknell University (in prep.).

Slaughter, Howard K. *George Fitzmaurice and his Enchanted Land.* Dublin: Dolmen, 1972.

Oliver St. John Gogarty (1878-1957)

COLLECTED AND SELECTED WORKS

Collected poems. Pref. by Yeats, AE, and Horace Reynolds. London: Constable, 1951. New York and Toronto: Longmans, Green, 1952.

The Plays of Oliver St. John Gogarty. Ed. James F. Carens. Newark, Del.: Proscenium, 1971. 500 copies.

Selected Poems. Fore. by AE and Horace Reynolds. New York: Macmillan, 1933. Same with title *Others to Adorn.* Pref. by Yeats. Fore by AE and Horace Reynolds. London: Rich and Cowan, 1938.

Unselected Poems. Baltimore: Contemporary Poetry, 1954.

INDIVIDUAL WORKS

PROSE

As I Was Going Down Sackville Street: A Phantasy in Fact. Intro. by Francis Hackett. London: Rich and Cowan; New York: Reynal and Hitchcock, 1937. Rev. ed. with title *As I Was Walking Down Sackville Street.* London: Rich and Cowan, 1939.

Blight: The tragedy of Dublin. An exposition in Facts by Alpha and Omega. Dublin: Talbot, 1917.

Going Native: The English are a queer folk with their lack of soul and their hard materialism, but they are a good people to live amongst. New York: Duell, Sloan, Pearce, 1940. London: Constable, 1941.

I Follow Saint Patrick. London: Rich and Cowan; New York: Reynal and Hitchcock, 1938. New ed., London: Constable; New York: Longmans, Green, 1950.

Intimations. Essays. New York: Abelard, 1950.

It Isn't This Time of the Year at All! An unpremeditated Autobiography. New York and Toronto: Doubleday; London: MacGibbon and Kee, 1954.

James Augustine Joyce. Dallas: The Times Herald, 1949.

Mad Grandeur: A novel. London and Toronto: Longmans, Green; New York and Philadelphia: Lippincott, 1941.

Mourning Becomes Mrs. Spendlove; and other portraits, grave and gay. New York: Creative Age, 1948.

Mr. Petunia. New York: Creative Age, 1945. London: Constable, 1946.

Rolling Down the Lea. London and New York: Constable, 1950.

Start from Somewhere Else: An exposition of wit and humour, polite and perilous. New York and Toronto: Doubleday, 1955.

Tumbling in the Hay: A novel. London: Constable; New York: Reynal and Hitchcock, 1939.

Week End in the Middle of the Week; and, other essays on the bias. Intro. by Ben Lucien Burman. New York: Doubleday, 1958.

William Butler Yeats: A memoir. Pref. by Myles Dillon. Dublin: Dolmen, 1963.

POETRY

Cervantes: Tercentenary of Don Quixote. Vice-Chancellor's English Verse Prize. Trinity College, Dublin, 1905 [Dublin, 1905].

Elbow Room; and other poems. Dublin: Cuala, 1939. New York: Duell, Sloan, and Pearce, 1942.

Hyperthuleana. Dublin: Walker, 1916. 25 numbered and signed copies.

An Offering of Swans; and other poems. Pref. by W. B. Yeats. Dublin: Cuala, 1923. 300 copies. London: Eyre and Spottiswoode [1924].

Others to Adorn. Pref. by W. B. Yeats. Fore. by AE and Horace Reynolds. London: Rich and Cowan, 1938.

Perennial: A new volume of poetry. Baltimore: Contemporary Poetry, 1944. London: Constable, 1946.

The Ship; and other poems. Dublin: Talbot, 1918.

Wild Apples. Dublin: Pvt. Ptd. at the Cuala, 1928. 250 copies. Same with intro. by W. B. Yeats. Dublin: Cuala, 1930. Same with title *Wild Apples. Poems.* Intro. by AE. New York and London: Cape and Smith, 1929.

INTRODUCTION BY

Defoe, Daniel. *The Fortunes and Misfortunes of the Famous Moll Flanders.* London: Temple, 1948.

Iris, Scharmel. *Bread Out of Stone.* Pref. by W. B. Yeats. Epilogue by Gogarty. Chicago: Regnery, 1953.

Ussher, Arlan. *The Face and Mind of Ireland*. Intro. New York: Devin-Adair, 1950.

LETTERS

Many Lines to Thee: Letters to G. K. A. Bell. Ed. by James F. Carens. Dublin: Dolmen, 1971.

CRITICAL AND BIOGRAPHICAL STUDIES

Jeffares, A. Norman. *Oliver St. John Gogarty*. London: Proceedings, 1960.
Lyons, J. B. *Oliver St. John Gogarty* (Irish Writers Series). Lewisburg, Pa.: Bucknell University (in prep.).

No author. *Farewell to the Senate*. London: Dixon [1935].

O'Connor, Ulick. *The Times I've Seen: Oliver St. John Gogarty. A biography*. New York: Obolensky, 1963. London: Cape, 1964.

Robert Graves (1895-   )

STANDARD BIBLIOGRAPHY

Higginson, Fred. H. *A Bibliography of the Works of Robert Graves*. London: Vane; Hamden: Shoe String, 1966.

POETRY

Colophon to Love Respelt. Barnet: Pvt. Ptd. for Robert Graves by Bill Hammerstone at the Stellar Press, 1967. 386 copies with 350 signed and numbered.

Love Respelt. Fore. London: Cassell, 1965. 250 signed and numbered copies and 30 unnumbered hors-commerce copies. Garden City: Doubleday, 1966.

*Poems about Love. Garden City: Doubleday, 1969.

Poems 1965-1968. London: Cassell, 1968. Garden City: Doubleday, 1969.

The Poor Boy Who Followed His Star; and 3 children's poems. London: Cassell, 1968; Garden City: Doubleday, 1969.

Seventeen Poems Missing from Love Respelt. Barnet: Pvt. Ptd. for Robert Graves by Bill Hammerstone at the Stellar Press, 1966. 330 signed and numbered copies.

Two Wise Children. New York: Quist, 1966. London: Allen, 1967.

Deyá: A portfolio of five poems and lithography by Robert Graves and Paul Hogarth. London: Motif Editions, 1972. Limited Edition.

Poems, Abridged for Dolls and Princes. London: Cassell, 1971. New York: Doubleday, 1972. Limited edition. "Enlarged facsimile edition of a miniature volume handwritten by the author for Queen Mary's dolls house (1922)."

Beyond Giving: Poems. Hatfield: Stellar, 1969. Distributor: London: Bertram Rota. 536 copies with 500 numbered, signed and for sale.

The Green-Sailed Vessel: Poems. Hatfield: Stellar, 1971. Distributor: London: Bertram Rota, 1971. 536 copies with 500 numbered and signed copies.

Timeless Meeting: Poems. Hatfield: Stellar, 1973. Distributor: London: Bertram Rota. 536 copies with 500 numbered, signed and for sale.

Poems, 1968-1970. London: Cassell, 1970. Garden City, New York: Doubleday, 1971.
Poems, 1970-1972. London: Cassell, 1972. Garden City, New York: Doubleday, 1973.

PROSE

Goodbye to All That. Abridged Edition. London: Cassell, 1966.

Difficult Questions, Easy Answers. London: Cassell, 1972. Garden City, New York: Doubleday, 1973.

The Crane Bag, and Other Disputed Subjects. London: Cassell, 1969.

On Poetry: Collected Talks and Essays. Garden City, New York: Doubleday, 1969.

The White Goddess—A Historical Grammar of Poetic Myth. Revised and Enlarged Edition. New York: Farrar, Straus & Giroux, 1966.

The Big Green Book. Illustrated by Maurice Sendak. New York: Crowell-Collier, 1968.

Greek Myths and Legends. Abr. ed. London: Cassell, 1968.

Poetic Craft and Principle: Lectures and Talks. Fore. London: Cassell, 1967.

INTRODUCTION BY

The Song of Songs. (fr. *Old Testament, The Song of Solomon*) Text and Introduction by Robert Graves. Illustrated by Hans Erni. London: Collins; New York: C. N. Potter, 1973.

Dalton, Catherine R. *Without Hardware*. Preface by Robert Graves. Canberra, Australia: Nicholson Prints & Publishing, 1970.

TRANSLATED BY

The Rubaiyyat of Omar Khayaam. A new trans. with critical commentaries by Robert Graves and Omar Ali-Shah. London: Cassell, 1967.

BIOGRAPHICAL AND CRITICAL STUDIES

Cohen, John Michael. *Robert Graves*. Edinburgh: Oliver and Boyd, 1960. New York: Grove, 1961.

Day, Douglas Turner, III. *Swifter than Reason: The poetry and criticism of Robert Graves*. Chapel Hill: University of North Carolina, 1963.

Enright, Dennis Joseph. *Robert Graves and the Decline of Modernism*. Inaugural lectured delivered on 17 November 1960 in the New Lecture Theatre . . . in the University of Malaya in Singapore. Singapore: University of Malaya, 1960.

Hoffman, Daniel C. *Barbarous Knowledge: Myth in the Poetry of Yeats, Graves, and Muir*. New York: Oxford University, 1967.

Kirkham, Michael. *The Poetry of Robert Graves*. London: Athlone; New York: Oxford University, 1969.

Seymour-Smith, Martin. *Robert Graves*. London and New York: Longmans, Green, 1956.

Stade, George. *Robert Graves*. New York and London: Columbia University, 1967.

Vickery, James B. *Robert Graves and the White Goddess*. Lincoln, Nebraska: University of Nebraska, 1972.

Lady Isabella Augusta Gregory (1852-1932)

COLLECTED WORKS

The Coole Edition. Ed. by T. R. Henn and Colin Smythe. Gerrards Cross, Buckinghamshire: Colin Smythe. New York: Oxford, 1969-1974.

Vol. I. *Visions and Beliefs in the West of Ireland*. With two essays and notes by W. B. Yeats and foreword by Elizabeth Coxhead. 1970.

Vol. II. *Cuchulain of Muirthemne: The Story of the Men of the Red Branch of Ulster*. With a preface by W. B. Yeats and foreword by Daniel Murphy. 1970.

Vol. III. *Gods and Fighting Men: The Story of the Tuatha DeNanaan and the Fianna of Ireland*. With preface by W. B. Yeats and foreword by Daniel Murphy. 1970.

Vol. IV. *Our Irish Theatre*. With a foreword by Roger McHugh. 1972.

Vol. V. *Collected Plays*. Vol. 1. *The Comedies*. All four volumes of *Collected Plays* ed. by Ann Saddlemyer. In preparation.

Vol. VI. *Collected Plays*. Vol. 2. *Tragedies and Tragic Comedies*. 1970.

Vol. VII. *Collected Plays*. Vol. 3. *Wonder and Supernatural*. 1970.

Vol. VIII. *Collected Plays*. Vol. 4. *Translations, Adaptations and Collaborations*. 1970.

Vol. IX. *The Kiltartan Books*. With a foreword by Padraic Colum. 1971.

Vol. X. *Hugh Lane: His Life & Legacy*. With a foreword by Padraic Colum. 1973.

Vol. XI. *Poets and Dreamers*. With a foreword by T. R. Henn. 1974.

Vol. XII. *A Book of Saints and Wonders*. With a foreword by Edward Malins. 1971.

Vol. XIII. *Seventy Years. An autobiography*. With a foreword by Colin Smythe. In preparation.

Vol. XIV. *The Journals*. In preparation.

Vol. XV. *The Journals*. In preparation.

Vol. XVI. *Sir William Gregory: An Autobiography*. Ed. by Lady Gregory with a foreword by Raymond Lister. In preparation.

Vol. XVII. *Mr. Gregory's Letter Box 1813-1835.* Ed. by Lady Gregory with a foreword by Jon Stallworthy. In preparation.

Vol. XVIII. *Shorter Prose Writings.* Vol. 1. With a foreword by D. J. Gordon. In preparation.

Vol. XIX. *Shorter Prose Writings* Vol. 2. In preparation.

Vol. XX. *The Lectures of Lady Gregory.* In preparation.

Vol. XXI. *A Catalogue of Sir William and Lady Gregory's Libraries at Coole, A Bibliography of Lady Gregory's Writings and a General Index to the Coole Edition.* With an intro. by Kathleen Raine. In preparation.

SELECTED PLAYS

The Image; and other plays. London and New York: Putnam, 1922. Also in separate issue: *The Image, The Wrens, Shanwalla, Hanrahan's Oath.*

Irish Folk-History Plays. 2 vols. New York and London: Putnam, 1912.

Lady Gregory's Irish Plays. Dublin: Talbot; London: Putnam, 1918. Also in separate issue: *Spreading the News, Hyacinth Halvey, The Rising of the Moon, the Jackdaw, The Workhouse Ward, The Travelling Man, The Gaol Gate.*

New Comedies. Notes. London and New York: Putnam, 1913. Also in Separate issue: *Coats, The Full Moon, The Bogie Men, Damer's Gold, McDonough's Wife.*

Selected Plays. Chosen with an intro. by Elizabeth Coxhead. Fore. by Sean O'Casey. London: Putnam, 1962. New York: Hill and Wang, 1963.

Seven Short Plays. Musical notes. Dublin: Maunsel, 1909. London and New York: Putnam [1923]. Also in separate issue in 1910: *Spreading the News, Hyacinth Halvey, The Rising of the Moon, The Jackdaw, The Workhouse Ward, The Travelling Man, the Gaol Gate.*

Spreading the News, The Rising of the Moon by Lady Gregory, The Poorhouse by Douglas Hyde. Dublin: Maunsel, 1906.

Three Last Plays. Musical notes. London and New York: Putnam, 1928.

Three Wonder Plays. London and New York: Putnam, 1922. Also in separate issue: *The Dragon, Aristotle's Bellows, The Jester.*

INDIVIDUAL PLAYS

Aristotle's Bellows. See *Three Wonder Plays.*

Bogie Men: A comedy in one act. See *New Comedies.* New York and London: French, n.d.

Coats: A comedy in one act. See *New Comedies.* New York and London: French, n.d.

Damer's Gold: A comedy in two acts. See *New Comedies.* New York and London: French, n.d.

The Dragon: A wonder play in three acts. See *Three Wonder Plays.*

The Full Moon: A comedy in one act. Dublin: Pub. by the author at the Abbey Theatre, 1911. New York and London: French, n.d.

The Gaol Gate. See *Seven Short Plays* and *Lady Gregory's Irish Plays.* New York and London: French, n.d.

The Golden Apple: A play for Kiltartan children. London: Murray; New York and London: Putnam, 1916.

Hanrahan's Oath: A play. See *The Image; and other plays.* New York and London: French, n.d.

Hyacinth Halvey: A comedy. New York: Quinn, 1906. See *Seven Short Plays* and *Lady Gregory's Irish Plays.*

The Image: A play in three acts. Dublin: Maunsel, 1910. See *The Image; and other plays.* New York and London: French, n.d.

The Jackdaw: A farce in one act. Dublin: Maunsel, 1910. See *Seven Short Plays* and *Lady Gregory's Irish Plays.* New York and London: French, n.d.

The Jester: A play in three acts. See *Three Wonder Plays.*

Kincora: A play in three acts. Dublin: Maunsel; New York: Quinn, 1905. New York ed. of 50 numbered copies.

McDonough's Wife: A drama in one act. London and New York: French, n.d. See *New Comedies.*

My First Play. London: Mathews and Marot, 1930.

On the Racecourse: A play in one act. Dublin: Talbot; London: Putnam, 1922. New York and London: Putnam, 1926.

The Rising of the Moon. London: Putnam, 1907. Dublin: Maunsel, 1910. See *Seven Short Plays* and *Lady Gregory's Irish Plays.*

Shanwalla: A drama in three acts. New York and London: French, n.d. See *The Image; and other plays.*

Spreading the News. Dublin: Talbot (Maunsel); London: Putnam, 1909. See *Seven Short Plays* and *Lady Gregory's Irish Plays.*

The Story Brought by Brigid: A miracle play. Dublin: Maunsel, 1905. Same with title *The Story Brought by Brigid: A passion play in three acts.* London and New York: Putnam, 1923.

The Travelling Man: A morality in one act. Dublin: Maunsel, 1905. London: Putnam, 1909. See *Seven Short Plays* and *Lady Gregory's Irish Plays.*

The White Cockade: A comedy in three acts. Dublin: Maunsel, 1905.

Workhouse Ward: A farce in one act. See *Seven Short Plays* and *Lady Gregory's Irish Plays.* London and New York: French, 1959.

Wrens: A drama in one act. See *The Image; and other plays.*

BIOGRAPHICAL AND CRITICAL PROSE

Arabi and his Household. London: Paul and Trench, 1882.

A Book of Saints and Wonders. By Lady Gregory. According to the old writing and the memory of the people of Ireland. Dundrum: Dun Emer, 1906. 200 numbered copies. London: Murray, 1907. Same under title *The Voyages of St. Brendan the Navigator and Stories of Other Irish Saints.* London: Colin Smythe, 1973.

Case for the Return of Sir Hugh Lane's Pictures to Dublin. Pref. with letter by President Cosgrove. Dublin: Talbot, 1926.

Coole. Essays with introductory verse by W. B. Yeats. Dublin: Cuala, 1931.

Coole. Completed from the manuscript and edited by Colin Smythe. With a foreword by Edward Malins. "The 1931 edition contained III, IV and V chapters only of this text." Dublin: Dolmen, 1971. 1971.

Cuchulain of Muirthemne: The Story of the Red Men of Ulster. Arr. and Put into English. Pref. by W. B. Yeats. London :Murray, 1902.

Gods and Fighting Men: The Story of the Tuatha de Danaan and of the Fianna of Ireland. Arr. and put into English. Pref. by W. B. Yeats. London: Murray; New York: Scribner, 1904.

Hugh Lane's Life and Achievement. With some account of the Dublin Galleries. London: Murray; New York: Dutton, 1921.

Lady Gregory's Journals 1916-1930. Ed. by Lennox Robinson. London: Putnam, 1946. New York: Macmillan, 1947.

Our Irish Theatre: A chapter in autobiography. London and New York: Putnam, 1914. New York: Putnam, 1965. Same with an intro. by Daniel J. Murphy. New York: Capricorn, 1965.

Sir Hugh Lane's French Pictures. London: Chiswick, 1917.

Visions and Beliefs in the West of Ireland. Coll. and arr. Two Essays and notes by W. B. Yeats. 2 vols. London and New York: Putnam, 1920.

TRANSLATED BY

A Book of Saints and Wonders. Dundrum: Dun Emer, 1906. 200 numbered copies. London: Murray, 1907.

Goldoni, Carlo. *Mirandolina.* Dublin: Talbot; London and New York: Putnam; New York: French, 1924.

Hyde, Douglas. *Casadh an tSugáin; or, The Twisting of the Rope.* Baile Átha Cliath: An Cló-Chumann [1910]. Irish and English.

————. Dráma Breithe Chríosta. Baile Átha Cliath: An Cló-Chumann, n.d. Irish and English.

————. *Pleusgadh na bulgóide.* Baile Átha Cliath: Gill [1903]. Irish and English.

————. *Righ Seumas.* Átha Cliath: An Cló-Chumann [1904]. Irish and English.

The Kiltartan History Book. Dublin: Maunsel, 1909. London: Unwin, 1926.

The Kiltartan Poetry Book. Prose trans. from the Irish. Intro. Dublin: Cuala, 1918. London: Putnam, 1919.

The Kiltartan Wonder Book. Note. Dublin: Maunsel, 1910.

Molière. *The Kiltartan Molière.* Dublin: Maunsel, 1910.

Poets and Dreamers. Studies and trans. from the Irish. Dublin: Hodges, Figgis; London: Murray, 1903. Port Washington, N.Y.: Kennikat, 1967.

EDITED BY

Ideals in Ireland. Essays by AE, D. P. Moran, George Moore, Douglas Hyde, Standish O'Grady, and W. B. Yeats. London: At the Unicorn, 1901.

Irish Literature. Editor in chief, Justin MacCarthy; Associate Eds., Lady Gregory, Maurice F. Egan, Douglas Hyde; Managing ed., James Jeffrey Roche. 10 vols. Philadelphia: Morris, 1904. Chicago: De Bower-Elliott, 1904.

Mr. Gregory's Letter Box, 1813-1830. London: Smith, Elder, 1898.

Sir William Gregory: An autobiography with a portrait. Formerly Member of Parliament and sometime Governor of Ceylon. London: Murray, 1894.

JOINT AUTHOR

With W. B. Yeats. *Plays in Prose and Verse written for an Irish Theatre and generally with the help of a friend.* London: Macmillan, 1922.

————. *The Unicorn from the Stars; and other plays.* New York: Macmillan, 1908.

BIOGRAPHICAL AND CRITICAL STUDIES

Adams, Hazard. *Lady Gregory.* (Irish Writers Series). Lewisburg, Pa.: Bucknell University, 1973.

Coxhead, Elizabeth. *Lady Gregory: A Literary Portrait.* London and Toronto: Macmillan; New York: Harcourt, 1961.

————. *J. M. Synge and Lady Gregory.* London: Pub. for the British Council by Longmans, Green, 1962.

Gregory, Vere, R.T.M.A., LL.D. *The House of Gregory.* With a fore. by Thomas Ulick Sadlier, M.A., M.R.I.A. Dublin: Browne and Nolan, 1943.

*Gutsche, Thelma. *Selective Index to Hugh Lane's Life and Achievement by Lady Gregory.* Johannesburg: Johannesburg Public Library, 1964.

Klenze, Hilda Von. *Lady Gregory's Life and Work.* Bochum-Langendeer: Verlag Heinrich Poppinghaus O.H.Q., 1940.

Saddlemyer, Ann. *In Defense of Lady Gregory, Playwright.* Dublin: Dolmen, 1966.

F. R. Higgins (1896-1941)

POEMS

Arable Holdings: Poems. Dublin: Cuala, 1933. 300 copies.

The Dark Breed: A book of poems. London: Macmillan, 1927.

The Gap of Brightness: Lyrical poems. London and New York: Macmillan, 1940.

Island Blood: Poems. Fore. by AE. London: John Lane at the Bodley Head, 1925.

Salt Air. Dublin: Irish Bookshop, 1923. 500 copies.

EDITED BY AND INTRODUCTION

With W. B. Yeats. *Broadsides: A collection of old and new songs.* 1935. Songs by W. B. Yeats, James Stephens, F. R. Higgins, Frank O'Connor, Lyan Doyle, Bryan Guiness, Padraic Colum. Illus. by Jack B. Yeats, Victor Brown, Sean O'Sullivan, E. C. Peet, Harry Kernoff, Maurice McGonigal. Music by Arthur Duff. Fore. by W. B. Yeats and F. R. Higgins. Dublin: Cuala, 1935. Also issued singly in sheets each month. 300 copies.

McManus, M. J. *Connacht Songs.* Prefatory poem. Dublin: Talbot, 1927.

Neil, Crawford. *Happy Island: Child poems.* Pref. Dublin: Maire Nic Shiubhlaigh, 1916.

O'Connaire, Pádraic. *Field and Fair: Travels with a donkey in Ireland.* Trans. by Cormac Breathnach. Appreciation by F. R. Higgins. Dublin and Cork: Talbot, 1929.

Progress in Irish Printing. Ed. and with a fore. Dublin: Thom, 1936.

Douglas Hyde (1862-1949)

Items designated Hyde are listed in Padraig Ó Tailliur's "Ceartliosta de Leabhair, Paimfléid, etc. Foilsithe in Eirinn. Ag Connradh na Gaedhilge 1893-1918," *Comhar* (February-August, 1964).

PLAYS AND POEMS

An Cleamhnas (A Play). Baile Átha Cliath: An Cló-Chumann [1905]. Same with title *An Cleamhnas: An Craoibhín do sgríobh. An dara heagar.* Baile Átha Cliath: Oifig Díolta Foillseacháin Rialtais, 1934.

An Naomh ar Iarraidh. Baile Átha Cliath: Oifig Díolta Foillseacháin Rialtais, 1934.

An Pósadh: Dráma éin gnímh. Dublin: Gill, 1905.

Casadh an tSugáin; or, The Twisting of the Rope. Trans. by Lady Gregory. Baile Átha Cliath: Cló-Chumann [1905]. Irish and English. Same in Irish only with title *Casadh an tSugáin: Dráma aon Ghnímh. An chéad chluiche Gaedhilge do léirigheadh i nAmharclann. An dara h-eagar.* Baile Átha Cliath: Oifig Díolta Foillseacháin Rialtais, 1934.

Dráma Breith Chríosta. Trans. by Lady Gregory. Dublin: Gill, 1903. Irish and English. Same in Irish only with title *Breith Chríosta: Dráma aon-ghnímh.* Baile Átha Cliath: Oifig Díolta Foillseacháin Rialtais, 1935.

Fáith-Sgéal agus Óid do'n Oireachtas, 1901. Ó láimh An Chraoibhín Aoibhinn agus mallughadh an Bhóeir ar Schacsanaibh do rinne an Géagán Glas. An allegory. Dublin: The Irish Book Co., 1901. Irish and English.

Maístin an Bheurla. Baile Átha Cliath: Gill, 1913.

Pleusgadh na bulgóide; or, Bursting the Bubble. Trans. with illustrative notes by G. G. (Lady Gregory). Baile Átha Cliath: Gill [1903]. Irish and English. Same in Irish only with title *Pleusadh na bulgóide: Drama suilt i naon ghníomh.* Baile Átha Cliath: Oifig Díolta Foillseacháin Rialtais, 1934.

Righ Seumas; or, "King James." Trans. Lady Gregory. Átha Cliath: An Cló-Chumann [1904]. Irish and English. Same in Irish only with title *Righ Seumas.* Baile Átha Cliath: Oifig Díolta Foillseacháin Rialtais [1934].

Spreading the News, The Rising of the Moon by Lady Gregory. The Poorhouse by Lady Gregory and Douglas Hyde. Dublin: Maunsel, 1906.

Teach na mbocht. Dráma aon-ghnímh. Baile Átha Cliath: Oifig Díolta Foillseacháin Rialtais, 1934.

The Tinker and the Fairy. An Tincéar agus an tSidheóg: Dráma einghnímh. Trans. by Miss Butler. Dublin: Gill [1902]. Irish and English. Same in English only with title *The Tinker and the Fairy*. Music by M. Esposito. London: Breitkopf and Hartel, 1902. Same in Irish only with title *An Tincéar agus an tSidheóg: Dráma einghnímh*. Baile Átha Cliath: Oifig Díolta Foillseacháin Rialtais [1934].

Úbhla de'n Craoibh. Baile Átha Cliath: Gill [1900].

BIOGRAPHY, BIBLIOGRAPHY, AND CRITICISM BY

With D. J. O'Donoghue. *Catalogue of the Books and Manuscripts comprising the Library of the Late Sir John T. Gilbert*. Compiled by Douglas Hyde and D. J. O.Donoghue for the Corporation of the City of Dublin. Dublin: Browne and Nolan, 1918.

*The Gaelic League in Ireland to the Irish People in America. Dublin, 1911. Hyde 335.

*The Irish Language and Irish Intermediate Education: Dr. Hyde's Evidence. Dublin: Gill, 1901.

Irish Poetry: An essay in Irish with trans. in English and a vocabulary. Pub. for the Society for the Preservation of the Irish Language. Dublin: Gill, 1902.

The Last Three Centuries of Gaelic Literature. London: Pub. by the Irish Literary Society, 1894.

The Literary History of Ireland from the Earliest Times to the Present Day. London: Unwin; New York: Scribner's, 1899.

Mise agus an Connradh: Go dtí, 1905. Intro. Baile Átha Cliath: Oifig Díolta Foillseacháin Rialtais, 1937.

Mo Thurus go hAmerice; no, Imeasg na nGaedheal inr an Oilean Úr. Baile Átha Cliath: Oifig Díolta Foillseacháin Rialtais, 1937.

"The Necessity for De-Anglecising Ireland," The Revival of Irish Literature. Addresses by Sir Charles Gavan Duffy, Dr. George Sigerson, and Dr. Douglas Hyde. Ed. by Lady Gregory. London: Unwin [1918].

*Reply to Dr. Atkinson. Dublin: Gill, 1901.

Spain and England: Being an unpublished commentary by the late Dr. Douglas Hyde. Royal Leamington Spa: At the Sign of the Dove, 1955.

The Story of Early Gaelic Literature. Dublin: Sealy, Bryers, and Walker; London: Unwin; New York: Kenedy, 1895. Rev. ed., London: Unwin, 1920.

A University Scandal. Dublin: Eblana, 1939.

TRANSLATED BY

Abhráin atá Leagtha ar Reactúire; or, Songs ascribed to Raferty. Being the fifth chapter of "Songs of Connacht." Now for the first time coll. and trans. Baile Átha Cliath: Gill, 1903. Irish and English. Same in Irish only with twenty poems added and with title *Abhráin agus Dánta Reachtabhraigh.* Baile Átha Cliath: Oifig Díolta Foillseacháin Rialtais, 1933.

Abhráin Diadha chúige Connacht. The religious songs of Connacht: A collection of poems, stories, prayers, satires, ranns, charms, etc. 2 vols. Dublin: Gill; London: Unwin, 1905-1906. Same in Irish only with title *Abhráin Diadha chúige Connacht: Ar n-a gCur amach anois arís agus Tuilleadh abhrán léo.* Balie Átha Cliath: Oifig Díolta Foillseacháin Rialtais, 1937.

Abhráin Grádha chúige Connacht; or, Love Songs of Connacht: Being the fourth chapter of "Songs of Connacht." Now for the first time coll. and trans. Dublin: Gill; London: Unwin, 1893. Irish and English. Same in English only with title *Love Songs of Connacht.* Pref. by W. B. Yeats. Dundrum: Dun Emer, 1904. 300 copies. Same in Irish only with title *Abhráin gradha chúige Chonnacht.* Baile Átha Cliath: Oifig Díolta Foillseacháin Rialtais, 1933.

Amhráin Chúige Chonnacht: An leath-ran. The Songs of Connacht: The Half-Rann. Intro. Baile Átha Cliath: Lester, 1922. Irish and English.

Bancanna Tíre. Dublin: Irish Agricultural Organization Society, 1899. Irish and English.

Beside the Fire: A coll. of Irish Gaelic folk stories. Ed., trans., and annotated by Douglas Hyde with additional notes by Alfred Nutt. London: Nutt, 1890. Six tales from the above in Irish only with the title *Cois na Teineadh: Sgeulta Gaedheilge cruinnuighthe agus curtha le chéile le Dubhglas de h-Íde.* Dublin: Gill, n.d.

Dánta Éagsamhla agus Béarla curtha ortha ag Dubhglas de h-Íde. Miscellaneous Poems trans. into English. Dublin: Printed for the President of Ireland by Colm Ó Lochlainn at the Sign of the Three Candles, 1943.

Five Irish Stories. Trans. from the Irish of Sgeuluidhe Gaodhalach. Pref. Dublin: Gill [1896].

Four Irish Stories. From Part 2 of Sgeuluidhe Gaodhalach. Dublin: Gill [1898].

Gabháltais Shearluis Mhóir. The Conquests of Charlemagne. Ed. from the *Book of Lismore* and three other vellum MSS. Pref., trans., glossary, and notes. London: Irish Texts Society, 1917. Irish Texts Society, Vol. XIX. Irish and English.

Giolla an Fhiugha; or, The Lad of the Ferule. Eachtra Cloinne Righ na h-Ioruaidhe; or, The Adventures of the Children of the King of Norway. Ed. with trans., notes, and glossary. Pref. London: The Irish Texts Society, 1899. Irish Texts Society, Vol. I. Irish and English.

Legends of Saints and Sinners. Coll. and trans. from the Irish. Pref. Dublin: Talbot; London: Unwin; New York: Stokes, 1915.

Poems from the Irish. Ed. with an intro. by Monk Gibbon. Dublin: Figgis, 1963.

Prince Charlie and Flora. Trans. from the Scottish Gaelic. Dublin: Pvt. Ptd. at the Sign of the Three Candles, 1942.

Sgéalta Thomáis Uí Chathasaigh. Mayo stories told by Thomas Casey. Coll., ed., and trans. with notes. Pref. Dublin: Pub. for the Irish Texts Society by the Educational Co. of Ireland, 1939. Irish and English.

Sgéuluidhe Fior na Seachtmhaine. Pref. Baile Átha Cliath: Gill, 1911. Irish and English. Same in Irish only with pref. by the editor. Baile Átha Claith : Oifig Díolta Foillseacháin Rialtais, 1935.

Songs of St. Columcille. Fore. Dublin: Talbot, 1942.

The Three Sorrows of Story-telling; And ballads of St. Columkilla. Pref. London: Unwin, 1895. *The Three Sorrows* were reissued separately under these titles: *Deirdre: The First of The Three Sorrows of Story-telling.* Dublin: Talbot, 1939. *The Children of Lir: The second of The Three Sorrows of Story-telling.* Dublin: Talbot, 1940. *The Children of Tuireann: The Third of The Three Sorrows of Story-telling.* Dublin: Talbot, 1941.

EDITED BY AND INTRODUCTION

An Sgeuluidhe Gaedhealach. 3 vols. Baile Átha Cliath: Sealy, Bryers, and Walker, 1895. Same in 1 vol. in 1933. Partial issue in school ed. *Céithre Sgéulta Eile* (Sgéalta XI, XII, XIV, XIX). Baile Átha Cliath: Sealy, Bryers, and Walker; Dublin: Gill, 1898. *Céithre*

Sgéulta Eile (Sgéulta II, IV, V, VI). Baile Átha Cliath: Sealy, Bryers, and Walker; Dublin: Gill, 1898.

Every Irishman's Library. General eds.: Alfred Perceval Graves, William Magennis, Douglas Hyde. 12 vols. London and Leipsic: Unwin, 1914-1918.

Graves, Alfred Perceval. *The Irish Poems of Alfred Perceval Graves.* Pref. Dublin: Maunsel; London: Unwin, 1908.

Imtheachta an Oireachtais, 1900. Leabhar II. Trí Sgéalta. (Do Fuair an Chead Duais.) Baile Átha Cliath: Sealy, Bryers, and Walker [1902].

Irish Literature. Editor in chief, Justin McCarthy; Associate eds., M. F. Egan, D. Hyde, Lady Gregory, James Jeffrey Roche; Managing ed., Charles Walsh. 10 vols. Philadelphia, 1904.

Leabhar Sgeulaighteachta: Cruinnighthe agus curtha le chéile le Dúbhglas de h-Íde. Baile Átha Cliath: Gill, 1889. Same with 19 poems added. Baile Átha Cliath: Oifig Díolta Foillseacháin Rialtais, 1931.

*Lia Fáile Fidei Commisso Adam Boyd Simpson Medici: A journal for promoting the study of Irish language and literature. 1926.

Ó Chathasaigh, Thomáis. *Ocht Sgéalta Ó Choillte Maghach.* Baile Átha Cliath: An Chumainn le béaloideas Éireann ag Comhlacht oideachais na hÉireann, 1936.

*Pearse, Patrick Henry. *Amhrain Chuilm de Bhalis.* Pref. by Seosamh Laoide and Douglas Hyde. 1903. Hyde, 152.

Sigerson, George. *Bards of the Gael and Gall.* Dublin: Talbot; London: Unwin, 1925.

Taidhbhse an Chrainn. Vocabulary. Dublin: Cahill, 1915.

BIBLIOGRAPHICAL, BIOGRAPHICAL, AND CRITICAL STUDIES

Coffey, Diarmid. *Douglas Hyde: An Craoibhinn Aoibhinn.* Pref. Dublin: Maunsel, 1917.

———. *Douglas Hyde: President of Ireland.* Dublin and Cork: Talbot, 1938.

Daly, Dominic. *The Young Douglas Hyde: The Dawn of the Irish Revolution & Renaissance.* Totowa, N.J.: Rowman & Littlefield, 1974.

Dunleavy, Gareth. *Douglas Hyde.* (Irish Writers Series). Lewisburg, Pa.: Bucknell University [n.d.].

No author. *Caint do rinne An Craoibhin Aoibhinn: An a10 a Chlog Trathnana an 7adh la Meithim i láthair an Choisde Gnútha.* Dublin: n.p., [1913].

No author. *Teasbanadh Gradama don Craoibhin Aoidbhinn: Dr. Douglas Hyde. Appreciation of his services to the nation.* Dublin: Wood, 1934.

Denis Johnston (1901-   )

COLLECTED PLAYS

Collected Plays. Pref. and intro. to each play. 2 vols. London: Cape, 1960. Pub. in the U.S.A. in one vol. with title *The Old Lady Says "No!" and other plays.* Boston: Little, Brown, 1960.

The Golden Cuckoo; and other plays. Intro. London: Cape, 1954.

The Moon in the Yellow River and The Old Lady Says "No!"; Two plays. Fore. by C. P. Curran. London: Cape, 1932.

Storm Song and A Bride for the Unicorn: Two plays. London: Cape, 1935.

INDIVIDUAL PLAYS

The Moon in the Yellow River: A play in three acts. New York and Los Angeles: French, 1933. Same with title *The Moon in the Yellow River.* London: Cape, 1934. Rev. ed. Fore. by C. P. Currán. London: Cape, 1935.

CRITICAL PROSE

Dionysia. Mimeographed copy with inked corrections. 6 vols. According to Mr. Johnston, during 1949 and 1950 copies were given to various libraries.

In Search of Swift. Intro. Dublin: Hodges, Figgis, 1959.

John Millington Synge. New York and London: Columbia University, 1965.

Linea. Mimeographed sequel to *Dionysia* now being circulated to various libraries. 1967, rev. 1968.

Nine Rivers from Jordan: The chronicle of a journey and a search.
Introit. London: Verschoyle, 1953. Boston: Little, Brown, 1955.
Derek Verschoyle had this vol. edited from *Dionysia.*

JOINT AUTHOR

With Ernst Toller. *Blind Man's Bluff: A play in three acts.* London:
Cape, 1938.

With Hugo Weisgall. *Six Characters in Search of an Author.* Libretto by
Denis Johnston. Bryn Mawr, Pennsylvania: Merion Music; T.
Pressner, Sole agent, 1957.

BIOGRAPHY AND CRITICISM

Carens, James F. *Denis Johnston.* (Irish Writers Series). Lewisburg, Pa.:
Bucknell University [n.d.].

Ferrar, Harold. *Denis Johnston's Irish Theatre.* Dublin: Dolmen; New
York: Humanities, 1974.

James Joyce (1882-1941)

BIBLIOGRAPHY

Cohn, Alan M., and Kain, Richard M. "Supplemental JJ Checklist,
1962," *James Joyce Quarterly* (Winter 1964) I, 2, 15-22. Sub-
sequent lists, by Alan M. Cohn, appear under title "Supplemental JJ
Checklist, 19—," in the following issues of *James Joyce Quarterly*:
Checklist, 1963, *JJQ* (Fall, 1964) II, 1, 50-60; Checklist, 1964,
JJQ (Fall, 1965) III, 1, 50-61; Checklist, 1960-1961, *JJQ* (Winter,
1966) III, 2, 141-153; Checklist, 1959, *JJQ* (Spring, 1966) III,
3, 196-204; Checklist, 1965, *JJQ* (Winter, 1967) IV, 2, 120-130;
Checklist, 1966, *JJQ* (Fall, 1967) V, 1, 53-67; Checklist, 1967,
JJQ (Spring, 1969) VI, 3, 242-261; Checklist, 1968, *JJQ* (Spring,
1970) VII, 3, 229-250; Checklist, 1969, *JJQ* (Spring, 1971) VIII,
3, 236-256; Checklist, 1970, *JJQ* (Winter, 1973) X, 2, 240-261;
Checklist, 1971, *JJQ* (Winter, 1974) XI, 2, 150-164.

Deming, Robert H. *A Bibliography of James Joyce Studies.* Lawrence:
University of Kansas, 1964.

Slocum, John J., and Cahoon, Herbert. *A Bibliography of James Joyce,*
1882-1941. New Haven: Yale University, 1953.

RECENT PUBLICATIONS OF JOYCE'S WRITINGS

FICTION

The Cat and the Devil. Illus. by Richard Erdoes. New York: Dodd,
Mead, 1964. Same, illus. by Gerald Rose. London: Faber and
Faber, 1965.

Dubliners. The corrected text with an explanatory note by Robert
Scholes and fifteen drawings by Robin Jacques. London: Cape,
1967.

A First-Draft Version of Finnegans Wake. Ed. and annotated by David
Hayman. Austin: University of Texas; London: Faber and Faber,
1963.

Giacomo Joyce. Facsimiles and reduced reproductions. Intro. and notes
by Richard Ellmann. New York: Viking, 1968.

A Portrait of the Artist as a Young Man. Large type ed. The definitive
text, corrected from the Dublin holograph by Chester G. Henderson
and ed. by Richard Ellmann. New York: Viking, 1964.

Scribbledehobble. The ur-workbook for *Finnegans Wake.* Ed. with notes
and intro. by Thomas E. Connolly. Evanston: Northwestern University, 1961.

A Shorter Finnegans Wake. Ed. by Anthony Burgess. London: Faber
and Faber, 1966. New York: Viking, c1966, 1967.

Stephen Hero. Ed. from the ms in Harvard College Library by Theodore
Spencer. A new ed. incorporating the additional ms pages in the
Yale University Library and the Cornell University Library, ed. by
John J. Slocum and Herbert Cahoon. Norfolk, Conn.: New Directions, 1963. London: New English Library, 1966.

Topf! [Icarus 33 (March, 1961):2, according to headnote by Donald
Carroll, here first pub. from notebook. Rptd. as broadside.] London:
Turret Books, 1967.

Ulysses. "complete and unexpurgated; first American printing." Industry,
Cal.: Collectors Pub. [n.d.] [Facsimile rpt. of the 1960 Bodley
Head ed. minus the index, but plus many pp. of ads for sex books,
aid, etc. There is no t. p.; pub. info. taken from covers. 933 pp.]

PLAY

Exiles: A play in three acts. With the author's own notes and an intro. by Padraic Colum. London: Cape. New York: Viking, 1961.

LETTERS

Letters of James Joyce. Vol. I. Ed. with an intro. by Stuart Gilbert. London: Faber and Faber, 1957. Vols. II and III. Ed. with an intro. by Richard Ellmann. New York: Viking, 1966.

Selected Letters of James Joyce. Ed. with an intro. by Richard Ellmann. New York: Viking, 1975.

BIBLIOGRAPHICAL AND CRITICAL STUDIES ABOUT

Begnal, Michael and Eckley, Grace. *Narrator and Character in Finnegans Wake.* Lewisburg, Pa.: Bucknell University [n.d.].

Brown, Homer O. *James Joyce's Early Fiction: The Biography of a Form.* Cleveland: Press of Case Western Reserve, c. 1972, 1973.

Brown, Norman O. *Closing Time.* New York: Random House, 1973.

Burgess, Anthony. *Joysprick: An Introduction to the Language of James Joyce.* London: Deutsch, 1973.

Chace, William M., editor. *Joyce: A Collection of Critical Essays.* Englewood Cliffs, N.J.: Prentice-Hall, 1974.

Cixous, Helene. *The Exile of James Joyce.* Translated from French by Sally A. Purcell. New York: D. Lewis, 1972.

Daly, Leo. *James Joyce and the Mullingar Connection.* Dublin: Dolmen, 1974.

Deming, Robert H. *James Joyce: The Critical Heritage.* 2 vols. London: Routledge and K. Paul, 1970.

Ellmann, Richard. *Yeats and Joyce.* Dublin: Dolmen; London: Oxford University, 1967.

Envoy. Vol. 5, No. 17 (April 1951), James Joyce Edition. Ed. by John Ryan. Dublin.

Freund, Gisele and Carleton, Verna B. *James Joyce in Paris: His Final Years.* Preface by Simone de Beauvoir. New York: Harcourt, Brace and World, 1965.

Gifford, Don. *Notes for Joyce: An Annotation of James Joyce's Ulysses.* New York: Dutton, 1974.

Halper, Nathan. *The Early James Joyce*. New York: Columbia University, 1973.

Harmon, Maurice, ed. *James Joyce Symposium, 1st, Dublin, 1967*. Dublin: Dolmen; Dist. by Dufour, 1969.

Herring, Phillip F., editor. *Joyce's Ulysses notesheets in the British Museum*. Charlottesville, Va.: University Press of Virginia, 1972.

Lane, Gary, editor. *A Word Index to James Joyce's Dubliners*. Programmed by Roland Dedekind. New York: Haskell House, c. 1971, 1972. "Keyed to definitive 1968 Viking Press edition."

Litz, A. Walton. *James Joyce: A Literary Biography*. New York: Hippocrene Books, 1972.

Lyons, J. B. *James Joyce and Medicine*. Dublin: Dolmen; New York: Humanities, 1974.

*Miller-Budnitskaya, R. *James Joyce's Ulysses*. Folcroft, Pa.: Folcroft, 1973.

Power, Arthur R. *Conversations with James Joyce*. London: Millington, 1974.

San Juan, Epifanio, Jr. *James Joyce and the Craft of Fiction: An Interpretation of Dubliners*. Rutherford, N.J.: Fairleigh Dickinson, 1972.

*Schlauch, Margaret. *The Language of James Joyce*. Folcroft, Pa.: Folcroft, 1973.

Senn, Fritz, editor. *New Light on Joyce from the Dublin Symposium*. Bloomington, Ind.: Indiana University, 1972.

Steinberg, Edwin R. *The Stream of Consciousness and Beyond in Ulysses*. Pittsburgh, Pa.: University of Pittsburgh, 1973.

Patrick Kavanagh (1905-1967)

STANDARD BIBLIOGRAPHY

Kavanagh, Peter. *Garden of the Golden Apples. A bibliography of Patrick Kavanagh*. New York: Peter Kavanagh Handpress, 1972.

POEMS AND PROSE

Collected Poems. London: MacGibbon and Kee; New York: Devin-Adair, 1964. London ed. of 110 signed copies numbered I-X (hors commerce) and 1-100 (for sale).

*Collected Pruse. London: MacGibbon and Kee, 1967.

Come Dance with Kitty Stobling; and other poems. London: Longmans, 1960. Philadelphia: Dufour, 1964.

The Complete Poems of Patrick Kavanagh. Collected, arranged and edited by Peter Kavanagh. New York: Peter Kavanagh Handpress, 1972.

The Great Hunger: Poem. Dublin: Cuala, 1942. 250 copies. London: MacGibbon and Kee, 1967.

The Green Fool. London: Joseph, 1938. New York and London: Harper, 1939.

November Haggard. Uncollected prose and verse. Selected, arranged and edited by Peter Kavanagh. New York: Peter Kavanagh Handpress, 1971.

Ploughman and other poems. London: Macmillan, 1936.

Recent Poems. Pvt. ptd. in the U.S.A., 1958. 25 numbered and signed copies.

Self-Portrait. Dublin: Dolmen, 1964.

A Soul for Sale. Poems. London: Macmillan, 1947.

Tarry Flynn: A novel. London: Pilot; New York: Devin-Adair, 1949.

LETTERS

Lapped Furrows: Correspondence 1933-1967 between Patrick and Peter Kavanagh. With other documents. Ed. and with intro. by Peter Kavanagh. New York: Peter Kavanagh Handpress, 1969.

EDITED BY

Kavanagh's Weekly: A journal of literature and politics. Vol. 1-13. Dublin: Peter Kavanagh, 1952.

BIBLIOGRAPHY AND CRITICISM

O'Brien, Darcy. *Patrick Kavanagh.* (Irish Writers Series). Lewisburg, Pa.: Bucknell University (in prep.).

Warner, Alan. *Clay is the Word. Patrick Kavanagh, 1907-1967*. Dublin: Dolmen, 1974.

Benedict Kiely (1919-   )

FICTION

Call for a Miracle: A novel. London: Cape, 1950. New York: Dutton, 1951.

The Captain with the Whiskers. London: Methuen, 1960. New York: Criterion, 1961.

The Cards of the Gambler: A folktale. London: Methuen, 1953.

Dogs Enjoy the Morning: A novel. London: Gollancz, 1968.

Honey Seems Bitter. New York: Dutton, 1952. London: Methuen, 1954.

In a Harbour Green. London: Cape, 1949. New York: Dutton, 1950.

A Journey to the Seven Streams: Seventeen stories. London: Methuen, 1963.

Land Without Stars: A Novel. London: Johnson, 1946.

There Was an Ancient House. London: Methuen, 1955.

A Ball of Malt and Madame Butterfly. London: Gollancz, 1973.

NON-FICTION

Counties of Contention: A study of the origins and implications of the Partition of Ireland. Fore. Cork: Mercier, 1945.

Modern Irish Fiction: A critique. Dublin: Golden Eagle, 1950.

Poor Scholar: A study of the works and days of William Carleton, 1794-1869. London: Sheed and Ward, 1947. New York: Sheed and Ward, 1948.

INTRODUCTION BY

Mahler, James (ed.). *Sing a Song of Kickham: Songs of Charles J. Kickham; with Gaelic versions and musical notations*. Dublin: Duffy, 1965.

BIOGRAPHY AND CRITICISM

Casey, Daniel. *Benedict Kiely.* (Irish Writers Series). Lewisburg, Pa.: Bucknell University [n.d.]

Eckley, Grace. *Benedict Kiely.* New York: Twayne, 1972.

Thomas Kinsella (1928-   )

POEMS

Another September. Dublin: Dolmen, 1958. 50 numbered and signed copies and unlimited ed.

Butcher's Dozen: A lesson for octave of widgery. Dublin: Peppercanister, 1972.

Death of a Queen. Dublin: Dolmen, 1956.

Downstream. Dublin: Dolmen; London: Oxford University, 1962.

Finistere. Dublin: Dolmen, 1972.

Moralities: Poems. Dublin: Dolmen, 1960. 500 copies with 25 numbered and signed and 175 as The Dolmen Chapbook, Part 12.

New Poems 1973. Dublin: Dolmen, 1973.

Nightwalker; and other poems. Dublin: Dolmen; London: Oxford University; New York: Knopf, 1968.

Notes from the Land of the Dead and Other Poems. Dublin: Cuala, 1972. 500 copies. New York: Knopf (dist. by Random House), 1973.

Per Imaginem. Dublin: Dolmen, 1953. 25 copies.

Poems. Glengeary, Co. Dublin: Dolmen, 1956. 250 numbered copies with 1 to 50 signed.

Poems and Translations. New York: Atheneum, 1961.

A Selected Life. Dublin: Ptd. at Dolmen for Peppercanister, 1972.

Selected Poems. 1956-1968. Dublin: Dolmen; London: Oxford University, 1973.

The Starlit Eye: Verses. Dublin: Dolmen, 1952. 175 copies with 25 numbered and signed.

Tear: A poem. Cambridge, Mass.: Pym-Randall, 1969. 226 copies.

Three Legendary Sonnets. Dublin: Dolmen, 1952. 100 copies with 30 numbered and signed.

Wormwood. Dublin: Dolmen, 1966. 350 numbered and signed copies.

TRANSLATED BY

The Breastplate of Saint Patrick. Dublin: Dolmen, 1954. 275 numbered copies with 1-15 signed and 10 of these hors-commerce. Same with title *Faeth Fiadha.* Dublin: At the Dolmen by Commission, 1954. About 200 copies. Rev. trans. with title *Faeth Fiadha: The Breastplate of Saint Patrick.* 100 numbered copies and regular ed. Both in two bindings and two papers.

Longes Mac-n-Usnig: Being the Exile and Death of the Sons of Usnech. Trans. from the Book of Leinster. Dublin: Dolmen, 1954. 225 numbered copies with 1-25 signed.

The Tain. Trans. by Thomas Kinsella from the Irish, with brush drawings by Louis Le Brocquy. Dublin: Dolmen, 1969. Dolmen Eds. IX. Ed. of 1750 copies with 750 for sale in U.S.A. Dist. outside the Republic of Ireland by Oxford University Press and Irish University Press. Reg. ed. London, N.Y., Oxford University, 1970. Pub. in assoc. with the Dolmen Press, Dublin.

Thirty-three Triads. Trans. from the XII Century Irish. Dublin: Dolmen, 1957. 75 numbered and signed copies and 200 issued as The Dolmen Chapbook, Part IV.

EDITED BY

With John Montague. *The Dolmen Miscellany of Irish Writing.* Dublin: Dolmen; London: Oxford University, 1962.

The Search: Seventh Series. Pref. Carbondale: University of Southern Illinois, 1967.

The Search: Eighth Series. Pref. Carbondale: University of Southern Illinois, 1969.

JOINT AUTHOR

Poems by Thomas Kinsella, Douglas Livingstone, and Anne Sexton. London and New York: Oxford University, 1968.

Three Irish Poets: John Montague, Thomas Kinsella, Richard Murphy. A poetry reading presented by the Dolmen Press at the Royal Hibernian Hotel, Dublin, February 3, 1961. Dublin: Dolmen, 1961. 250 copies.

With W. B. Yeats. *Davis, Mangan, Ferguson? Tradition and the Irish Writer: Writings by W. B. Yeats and by Thomas Kinsella.* Dublin: Dolmen; dist. by Dufour, Chester Springs, Pa., 1970.

BIOGRAPHY AND CRITICISM

*Harmon, Maurice, *The Poetry of Thomas Kinsella.* Lewisburg, Pa.: Bucknell University, 1975.

Mary Lavin (1912-   )

FICTION

At Sallygap; and other stories. Boston: Little, Brown, 1947.

The Becker Wives; and other stories. London: Joseph, 1946.

Collected Stories. With an intro. by V. S. Pritchett. Boston: Houghton Mifflin, 1971.

The Great Wave; and other stories. London and New York: Macmillan, 1961.

Happiness and Other Stories. London: Constable, 1969. Boston: Houghton Mifflin, 1970.

The House in Clew Street. London: Joseph; Boston: Little, Brown, 1945.

In the Middle of the Fields; and other stories. London: Constable, 1967.

A Likely Story. New York: Macmillan, 1957. Dublin: Dolmen; London: Oxford University, 1967.

The Long Ago; and other stories. London: Joseph, 1944.

Mary O'Grady. London: Joseph; Boston: Little, Brown, 1950.

A Memory and Other Stories. London: Constable; Boston: Houghton Mifflin, 1973.

Patriot Son; and other stories. London: Joseph, 1956.

The Second Best Children in the World. Illus. by Edward Ardizzone. Boston: Houghton Mifflin; London: Longman Young Books, 1972.

Selected Stories. London and New York: Macmillan, 1959.

A Single Lady and Other Stories. London: Joseph, 1951.

The Stories of Mary Lavin. London: Constable; New York: Longmans, Green, 1964.

Tales from Bective Bridge. Boston: Little, Brown, 1942. Same with a pref. by Lord Dunsany. London: Joseph, 1943.

BIOGRAPHY AND CRITICISM

Bowen, Zack. *Mary Lavin.* (Irish Writers Series). Lewisburg, Pa.: Bucknell University (in prep.).

Donagh MacDonagh (1912-1968)

POEMS, PLAYS, PROSE

The Ballad of Jane Shore. Dublin: Dolmen, 1954. 250 copies.

The Celtic Master. Dublin: Dolmen, 1969.

The Course of Irish Verse in English. New York: Sheed and Ward, 1947. London: Sheed and Ward, 1948.

Happy as Larry: A play in verse. Dublin and London: Fridberg, 1946.

The Hungry Grass: Poems. London: Faber and Faber, 1947.

Information Please! Fore. London: Mellifont, 1944. Dublin: Pillar, 1945.

Ulysses Map of Dublin. (Dublin: Jame Joyce's Tower Committee 1962.) Donagh MacDonagh, c1963.

Veterans; and other poems. Dublin: Cuala, 1941. 270 numbered copies.

*A Warning to Conquerors. Pref. by Niall Sheridan. Dublin: Dolmen; London: Oxford University, 1968.

JOINT AUTHOR

With Niall Sheridan. *Twenty Poems*. Dublin: Pvt. ptd., 1934. 300 numbered copies with 30 signed.

EDITED BY

Letters of People in Love. Comp. by Donagh MacDonagh. London: Mellifont [1944].

Poems from Ireland: An anthology of poems published in The Irish Times. Ed. with an intro. Pref. by R. M. Smyllie. Dublin: Irish Times, 1944.

With Lennox Robinson. *The Oxford Book of Irish Verse: XVIIth Century–XXth Century*. Pref. by Lennox Robinson. Intro. by Donagh MacDonagh. Oxford: Clarendon, 1958.

Thomas MacDonagh (1878-1916)

PLAYS AND POEMS

April and May; with other verse. Dublin: Sealy, Bryers, and Walker [1904].

The Golden Joy. Dublin: O'Donoghue; Gill, 1906.

Lyrical Poems. Dublin: The Irish Review, 1913. 500 copies.

Pagans: A modern play in two conversations. Dublin: Talbot; London: Unwin, 1920.

Poems by Thomas MacDonagh: Selected by his sister. Dublin: Talbot [1925].

The Poetical Works of Thomas MacDonagh. Ed. with an intro. by James Stephens. Dublin: Talbot; London: Unwin, 1916. New York: Stokes, 1917.

Songs of Myself. Dublin: Hodges, Figgis, 1910.

Through the Ivory Gate: A book of verse. Dublin: Sealy, Bryers, and Walker [1903].

When the Dawn Is Come: A tragedy in three acts. Dublin: Maunsel, 1908.

CRITICAL AND HISTORICAL

In Memoriam. Last and inspiring address of Thomas MacDonagh. Dublin: Pvt. ptd. at Cuala for Kilkelly, 1916.

Literature in Ireland: Studies in Irish and Anglo-Irish. Dublin: Talbot; London: Unwin, 1916. Same with intro. by Daniel Corkery in 1939.

Thomas Campion and the Art of English Poetry. Pref. Dublin: Hodges, Figgis; London: Simpkin and Marshall, 1913.

CRITICAL AND BIBLIOGRAPHICAL STUDIES

Parks, Edel Winfield, and Aileen Wells. *Thomas MacDonagh: The Man, the Patriot, the Writer.* Athens: University of Georgia, 1967.

Sheehy-Skeffington, Francis. *An Open Letter to Thomas MacDonagh.* Dublin: n.p., n.d. Rpd. from "The Irish Citizen" of May 22, 1915, by the Irishwoman's International League.

Michael McLaverty (1907-   )

FICTION

The Brightening Day: A novel of Ireland. London: Collier-Macmillan; New York: Macmillan, 1965.

Call My Brother Back: A novel. London, New York, Toronto: Longmans, 1939.

Choice. London: Cape; New York: Macmillan, 1958.

The Game Cock; and other stories. London: Allen; New York: Devin-Adair, 1947.

In This Thy Day. London: Cape, 1945. New York: Macmillan, 1947.

Lost Fields. New York and Toronto: Longmans, 1941. London: Cape, 1942.

School for Hope. London: Cape; New York: Macmillan, 1954.

The Three Brothers. London: Cape; New York: Macmillan, 1948.

Truth in the Night. New York: Macmillan, 1951. London: Cape, 1952.

White Mare; and other stories. Newcastle, County Down, Northern Ireland: Mourne, 1943.

Louis MacNeice (1907-1963)

STANDARD BIBLIOGRAPHY

Armitage, C. M. and Clark, Neil. *A Bibliography of the Works of Louis MacNeice.* London: Kaye and Ward, 1973.

COLLECTED AND SELECTED POEMS

Collected Poems, 1925-1948. London: Faber and Faber; New York: Oxford University, 1949.

Collected Poems of Louis MacNeice. Ed. by E. R. Dodds. London: Faber and Faber, 1966. New York: Oxford University, 1967.

Eighty-five Poems. Sel. by MacNeice. London: Faber and Faber; New York: Oxford University, 1959.

Holes in the Sky: Poems, 1944-1947. London: Faber and Faber, 1948. New York: Random House, c. 1948, 1949.

Poems. London: Faber and Faber, 1935. New York: Random House, 1937.

Poems, 1924-1940. New York: Random House, 1940.

Selected Poems. London: Faber and Faber, 1940.

Selected Poems. Sel. with an intro. by W. H. Auden. London: Faber and Faber, 1964.

Springboard: Poems, 1941-1944. London: Faber and Faber, 1944. New York: Random House, 1945.

INDIVIDUAL VOLUMES OF POEMS

Autumn Journal: A poem. London: Faber and Faber; New York: Random House, 1939.

Autumn Sequel: A rhetorical poem in XXVI cantos. London: Faber and Faber, 1954.

Blind Fireworks: Poems. London: Gollancz, 1929.

The Burning Perch. London: Faber and Faber; New York: Oxford University, 1963.

The Earth Compels: Poems. London: Faber and Faber, 1938.

The Last Ditch: Poems. Dublin: Cuala, 1940. 450 numbered copies with 1-25 signed.

The Other Wing. London: Faber and Faber [1954].

Plant and Phantom: Poems. London: Faber and Faber, 1941.

Solstices: Poems. London: Faber and Faber; New York: Oxford University, 1961.

Ten Burnt Offerings: Poems. London: Faber and Faber, 1952. London and New York: Oxford University, 1953.

Visitations: Poems. London: Faber and Faber, 1957. London and New York: Oxford University, 1958.

PROSE

Astrology. Ed. Douglas Hill. London: Aldus; Garden City, N.Y.: Doubleday, 1964.

I Crossed the Minch: An account of travel in the Outer Hebrides. New York, London, and Toronto: Longmans, Green, 1938.

Meet the U.S. Army. Prepared for the Board of Education by the Ministry of Information. London: His Majesty's Stationery Office, 1943.

Modern Poetry: A personal essay. Pref. London: Oxford University, 1938. New York: Oxford University, 1939.

Penny That Rolled Away. London: Allen; New York: Putnam, 1954.

The Poetry of W. B. Yeats. London, New York, and Toronto: Oxford University, 1941. Same with a fore. by Richard Ellmann. London: Faber and Faber, 1967.

Sixpence That Rolled Away. London: Faber and Faber, 1964.

The Strings Are False: An unfinished autobiography. Ed. with a pref. by E. R. Dodds. London: Faber and Faber, 1965.

Varieties of Parable. Clarke Lectures, 1963. Cambridge: Cambridge University, 1965.

Zoo. London: Joseph, 1938.

PLAYS

Christopher Columbus: A radio play. London: Faber and Faber [1934].

The Dark Tower; and other radio scripts. London: Faber and Faber, 1947.

The Mad Islands and The Administrator. Two radio plays. London: Faber and Faber; New York: Oxford University, 1964.

One for the Grave: A Modern Morality Play. London: Faber and Faber; New York: Oxford University, 1968.

Persons from Porlock and Other Plays for Radio. With intro. by W. H. Auden. London: British Broadcasting Corp., 1969.

TRANSLATED BY

The Agamemnon of Aeschylus. Pref. London: Faber and Faber, 1936. New York: Harcourt, 1937.

Goethe's Faust: Parts I and II. An abridged version. London: Faber and Faber; New York: Oxford University, 1951.

JOINT AUTHOR

With W. H. Auden. *Letters from Iceland: In prose and verse.* Pref. London: Faber and Faber; New York: Random House, 1937.

UNDER THE PSEUDONYM OF LOUIS MALONE

Out of the Picture: A play in two acts. London: Faber and Faber, 1937. New York: Harcourt, 1938.

Roundabout Way: A novel. London and New York: Putnam, 1932.

EDITED BY

With Bonamy Dobree and Philip Larkin. *New Poems, 1958.* London: Joseph, 1958.

With Stephen Spender. *Oxford Poetry.* Oxford: Blackwell, 1929.

CRITICAL STUDIES

Auden, Wystan Hugh. *Louis MacNeice: A memorial address.* Delivered at All Souls, Langham Place on 17 October 1963. London: Pvt. ptd. for Faber and Faber, 1963.

McKinnon, William T. *Apollo's Blended Dream: A Study of the Poetry of Louis MacNeice*. London and New York: Oxford University, 1971.

Moore, Donald Bert. *The Poetry of Louis MacNeice*. Leicester: Leicester University, 1972.

Press, John. *Louis MacNeice*. London: Pub. for the British Council and the National Book League by Longmans, Green, 1965. Writers and Their Work, No. 187.

Smith, Edward Elton. *Louis MacNeice*. New York: Twayne, 1970.

Ethel Mannin (1900-   )

FICTION

All Experience. London: Jarrolds, 1932.

Ann and Peter in Austria. London: Muller, 1962.

Ann and Peter in Japan. London: Muller, 1960.

Ann and Peter in Sweden. London: Muller, 1959.

At Sundown, The Tiger. London and New York: Jarrolds; New York: Putnam, 1951.

Bavarian Story. London: Jarrolds [1949]. New York: Appleton-Century-Crofts, 1950.

Bitter Babylon. London: Hutchinson, 1968.

The Blossoming Bough. London and New York: Jarrolds [1943].

The Blue-eyed Boy. London: Jarrolds, 1959.

Bruised Wings; and other stories. London: Wright and Brown [1931].

The Burning Bush. London: Hutchinson, 1965.

Cactus. London: Jarrolds, 1935. Rev. ed., Harmondsworth and New York: Penguin, 1941.

Captain Moonlight. London: Jarrolds [1942].

Children of the Earth. London: Jarrolds [1930]. Garden City, New York: Doubleday, 1930.

Comrade, O Comrade; or, Lowdown on the left. London and New York: Jarrolds [1947].

Crescendo: Being the dark odyssey of Gilbert Stroud. London: Jarrolds [1928]. Garden City, N.Y.: Doubleday, 1929.

The Curious Adventure of Major Fosdick. London: Hutchinson, 1972.

The Dark Forest. London: Jarrolds [1946].

Darkness My Bride. London: Jarrolds [1936].

Dryad. Author's note. London: Jarrolds [1933].

Every Man a Stranger. London: Jarrolds [1950].

The Falconer's Voice. Author's Note. London: Jarrolds [1935].

The Fields at Evening. London: Jarrolds, 1952.

Fragrance of Hyacinths. London: Jarrolds, 1958.

Free Pass to Nowhere. London: Hutchinson, 1970.

Green Figs. Tales. London: Jarrolds [1931].

Green Willow. London: Jarrolds [1928]. Garden City, New York: Doubleday, 1928.

Hunger of the Sea. London: Jarrolds; New York: Duffield, 1924.

Julie: The Story of a dance-hostess. London: Jarrolds [1940].

Kildoon. London: Hutchinson, 1974.

The Lady and the Mystic. London: Hutchinson, 1967.

Late Have I Loved Thee. London: Jarrolds [1948]. New York: Putnam, 1948.

Linda Shawn. London: Jarrolds; New York: Knopf, 1932.

Living Lotus. London: Jarrolds; New York: Putnam, 1956.

Lover Under Another Name. London: Jarrolds [1953]. New York: Putnam, 1954.

Love's Winnowing. London: Wright and Brown [1932].

Lucifer and the Child. Author's note. London: Jarrolds [1945].

Martha: A novel. London: Parsons; New York: Duffield, 1923. Rev. ed., London: Jarrold's, 1929.

Men Are Unwise. London: Jarrolds; New York: Knopf, 1934.

The Midnight Street. London: Hutchinson, 1969.

Mission to Beirut. London: Hutchinson, 1973.

My Cat Sammy. Photographs by F. W. Ziemsen. London: Joseph, 1971.

*The Night and Its Homing. London: Hutchinson, 1966.

No More Mimosa. Author's note. London: Jarrolds [1943].

Pilgrims. London: Jarrolds [1927]. New York: Doran, 1927.

Pity the Innocent. London: Jarrolds; New York: Putnam, 1957.

Proud Heaven. London: Jarrolds [1944].

The Pure Flame. London: Jarrolds, 1936.

Ragged Banners: A novel with an index. London: Jarrolds [1931]. New York: Knopf, 1931.

Red Rose: A novel based on the life of Emma Goldman. London: Jarrolds [1941].

The Road to Beersheba. London: Hutchinson, 1963. Chicago: Regnery, 1964.

Rolling in the Dew. London: Jarrolds [1940].

Rose and Sylvie. Note. London: Jarrolds [1938].

Sabishisa. London: Hutchinson, 1961.

The Saga of Sammy-cat. New York: [Oxford University] Pergamon, 1969.

Selected Stories. Dublin and London: Fridberg, 1946.

Sleep After Love. London: Jarrolds, 1942.

So Tiberius. London: Jarrolds, 1954. New York: Putnam, 1955.

Sounding Brass. London: Jarrolds, 1925. New York: Duffield, 1926.

Tinsel Eden; and other stories. London: Wright and Brown [1931].

Venetian Blinds. London: Jarrolds; New York: Knopf, 1933.

The Wild Swans; and other tales based on the ancient Irish. London: Jarrolds, 1952.

Women Also Dream. London: Jarrolds; New York: Putnam, 1937.

NON-FICTION

An American Journey. London: Hutchinson, 1967.

Aspects of Egypt: Some travels in the United Arab Republic. London: Hutchinson, 1964.

Bread and Roses: An utopian survey and blue-print. London: Macdonald, 1944.

Brief Voices: A writer's story. London: Hutchinson, 1959.

Castles in the Street. London and Letchwood: Dent [1942].

Christianity—or Chaos? A re-statement of religion. London: Jarrolds [1940].

Commonsense and Morality. Pref. by A. S. Neill. London and New York: Jarrolds [1942].

Commonsense and the Adolescent. Pref. by A. S. Neill. London: Jarrolds [1937]. Rev. ed. [1945].

Commonsense and the Child: A plea for freedom, etc. Pref. by A. S. Neill. London: Jarrolds, 1931. Philadelphia and London: Lippincott, 1932.

Confessions and Impressions. London: Jarrolds, 1930. Rev. ed., London: Hutchinson, 1936.

Connemara Journal. London: Westhouse, 1947.

The Country of the Sea: Some wanderings in Brittany. London: Jarrolds, 1957.

Curfew at Dawn. London: Hutchinson, 1962.

England at Large. London: Hutchinson, 1970.

England for a Change. London: Hutchinson, 1968.

England My Adventure. London: Hutchinson, 1972.

The Flowery Sword. Travels in Japan. London: Hutchinson, 1960.

Forever Wandering: Impressions of travel. London: Jarrolds, 1934. New York: Dutton, 1935.

German Journey. London: Jarrolds [1950].

Jungle Journey. London: Jarrolds [1950].

A Lance for the Arabs: A Middle East journey. London: Hutchinson, 1963.

Land of the Crested Lion: A journey through modern Burma. London: Jarrolds, 1955.

Loneliness: A study of the human condition. London: Hutchinson, 1966.

The Lovely Land: The Hashemite Kingdom of Jordan. London: Hutchinson, 1965.

Moroccan Mosaic. London: Jarrolds, 1953.

Practitioners of Love. London: Hutchinson, 1969. New York: Horizon, 1970.

Privileged Spectator: A sequel to Confessions and Impressions. London: Jarrolds, 1939. Rev. ed. [1948].

Rebel's Ride: A consideration of the revolt of the individual. London: Hutchinson, 1964.

South of Samarkand. London: Jarrolds, 1936. New York: Dutton, 1937.

This Was a Man: Some memories of Robert Mannin by his daughter Ethel Mannin. London: Jarrolds, 1952.

Two Studies in Integrity: Gerald Griffin and the Rev. Francis Mahoney. London: Jarrolds; New York: Putnam, 1954.

With Will Adams Through Japan. London: Muller, 1962.

Women and the Revolution. London: Secker and Warburg, 1938. New York: Dutton, 1939.

Young in the Twenties: A Chapter of Autobiography. London: Hutchinson, 1971.

Edward Martyn (1859-1923)

PLAYS

The Dream Physician: A play in five acts. Dublin: Talbot; London: Unwin; London: Duckworth [1918].

Grangecolman: A domestic drama in three acts. Dublin: Maunsel, 1912.

The Heatherfield: A play in three acts. London: Duckworth; New York: Brentano's [1917].

The Heatherfield and Maeve: Two plays. Intro. by George Moore. London: Duckworth, 1899.

Maeve: A psychological drama in two acts. London: Duckworth; New
York: Brentano's [1917].

FICTION

The Tale of a Town and An Enchanted Sea. London: Unwin; Kilkenny:
O'Grady, 1902.

UNDER THE PSEUDONYM OF SIRIUS

Morgante the Lesser: His notorious life and wonderful deeds. Arr. and
narrated for the first time. Pref. London: Swan and Sonnenschein,
1890.

CRITICISM

Ireland's Battle for Her Language. Dublin: Gaelic League, n.d.

PREFACE

Elliot, Robert. *Art and Ireland.* Dublin: Sealy, Bryers, and Walker
[1906].

O'Hanlon, Henry B. *The All-alone: A play in four acts.* Dublin: Kiersay
[1919].

BIOGRAPHICAL AND CRITICAL STUDIES

Courtney, Sister Marie Therese. *Edward Martyn and the Irish Theatre.*
Pref. Hollywood and Washington, D.C.: Vantage, 1956.

Gwynn, Denis Rolleston. *Edward Martyn and the Irish Revival.* Intro.
London: Cape, 1930.

Setterquist, Jan. *Ibsen and the Beginnings of Anglo-Irish Drama: II.*
Edward Martyn. Pref. Upsala: Lundequist; Cambridge, Mass.;
Harvard; Dublin: Hodges, Figgis, 1960.

Rutherford Mayne, pseud. of Samuel Waddell (1878- ?)

PLAYS

Bridgehead: A play in three acts. Note. London: Constable, 1939.

The Drone: A play in three acts. Dublin: Maunsel, 1909.

The Drone; and other plays. Dublin: Maunsel, 1912.

Peter: A comedy in three acts and a prologue. Dublin: Duffy, 1944.

The Troth: A play in one act. Dublin: Maunsel, 1909.

The Turn of the Road: A play in two scenes and an epilogue. Dublin: Maunsel, 1907.

Ewart Milne (1903-   )

POEMS

Boding Day. London: Muller, 1947.

Diamond Cut Diamond: Selected Poems. London: Bodley Head, 1953.

Elegy for a Lost Submarine. Burnham-on-Crouch: Plow Poems, 1951.

Forty North Fifty West: Poems. Dublin: Gayfield, 1938. 250 copies.

Galion: A Poem. Dublin: Dolmen, 1953. 24 signed and numbered copies.

A Garland for the Green: Poems. London: Hutchinson, 1962.

Jubilo: Poems. London: Muller, 1944.

Letter from Ireland: Verses. Dublin: Gayfield, 1940.

*Life Arboreal: Poems. Tunbridge Wells: Pound, 1953.

Listen Mangan: Poems. Dublin: The Sign of the Three Candles, 1941.

Once More to Tourney: A book of ballads and light verse, serious, gay, and grisly. Intro. by J. M. Cohen. London: Linden, 1958.

Time Stopped: A poem-sequence with prose intermissions. London: Plow Poems, 1967.

John Montague (1929-   )

POETRY

All Legendary Obstacles. Dublin: Dolmen, 1966. 300 signed copies.

The Bread God. Dublin: Dolmen, 1968. 250 signed and numbered copies with 1-150 hors-commerce.

A Chosen Light. London: MacGibbon and Kee, 1967. Chicago: Swallow, 1969.

Forms of Exile. Poems. Dublin: Dolmen, 1958.

*The Golden Stone. Cork: Golden Stone, 1974.

Home Again. Belfast: Festival Publications, 1967.

Hymn to the New Omagh Road. Dublin: Pvt. ptd. at the Dolmen, 1968. 175 signed copies.

A New Siege: A folder of a section of The Rough Field. Dublin: Dolmen, 1970.

*The Old People. According to Brian Cleeve, this book was privately printed in Dublin in 1960.

Patriotic Suite. Dublin: Dolmen, 1966. 1000 copies with 100 signed and numbered.

Poisoned Lands; and other poems. London: MacGibbon and Kee, 1961. Chester Springs: Dufour, 1963.

The Rough Field, 1961-1971. Dublin: Dolmen, 1972.

Tides. Dublin: Dolmen; Dist. by Oxford University Press, 1970. Chicago: Swallow, 1971.

FICTION

Death of a Chieftain; and other stories. London: MacGibbon and Kee, 1967. Chester Springs: Dufour, 1968.

JOINT AUTHOR

Three Irish Poets: John Montague, Thomas Kinsella, Richard Murphy. A poetry reading presented by the Dolmen Press at the Royal Hibernian Hotel, Dublin, Feb. 3, 1961. Dublin: Dolmen, 1961. 250 copies.

EDITED BY

The Faber Book of Irish Verse. London: Faber and Faber, 1974.

With Thomas Kinsella. *The Dolmen Miscellany of Irish Writing*. Dublin: Dolmen; London: Oxford University, 1962.

With Liam Miller. *A Tribute to Austin Clarke on His Seventieth Birthday, 9 May 1966*. Dublin: Dolmen, 1966.

TRANSLATED BY

A Fair House. Dublin: Cuala, 1974.

CRITICAL WORKS ABOUT

Kersnowski, Frank. *John Montague.* (Irish Writers Series). Lewisburg,
Pa.: Bucknell University, 1975.

Brian Moore (1921-   )

FICTION

An Answer From Limbo. Boston and Toronto: Little, Brown, 1962.
London: Deutsch, 1963.

Catholics. London: Cape, 1972; New York: Holt, Rinehart & Winston,
1973.

The Emperor of Ice-cream. A novel. New York: Viking, 1965. London:
Deutsch, 1966.

The Feast of Lupercal. London: Deutsch; Boston and Toronto: Little,
Brown, 1957. Same with title *A Moment of Love.* London: Panther,
1966.

Fergus. New York: Holt, Rinehart & Winston, 1970. London: Cape,
1971.

The Great Victorian Collection. New York: Farrar, Straus & Giroux,
1975.

I Am Mary Donne. A novel. New York: Viking, 1968.

Judith Hearne. London: Deutsch, 1955. Same with title *The Lonely
Passion of Miss Judith Hearne.* Harmondsworth: Penguin, 1959.
Same with title *The Lonely Passion of Judith Hearne.* Boston:
Little, Brown, c1955, 1956. Same with title *Judith Hearn.* Intro. by
John Stedmond. Toronto: McClelland and Stewart, 1964.

The Luck of Ginger Coffey: A novel. London: Deutsch; Boston and
Toronto: Little, Brown, 1960.

The Revolution Script. Toronto: McClelland and Stewart, 1971. New
York: Pocket Books, 1972.

NON-FICTION

With the Editors of *Life. Canada.* New York: Time, 1963. Rev. ed. New York: Time, 1968.

BIOGRAPHY AND CRITICISM

Dahlie, Hallvard. *Brian Moore.* Toronto: Copp Clark, 1969.
Flood, Jeanne. *Brian Moore.* Lewisburg, Pa.: Bucknell University [n.d.].

George Moore (1852-1933)

BIBLIOGRAPHY

Gilcher, Edwin. *A Bibliography of the Writings of George Moore.* De-kalb: Northern Illinois University, 1970.

Williams, Iolo A. *George Moore: A bibliography.* Pref. letter by Moore. London: Chaundy, 1921.

Gerber, Helmut E. *George Moore: An annotated bibliography of writings about him. English Literature in Transition.* Part One, II, No. 2 (1959); Part Two, II, No. 3 (1959), whole issues. Supplement I, III, No. 2 (1960), 34-36. Supplement II, IV, No. 2 (1961), 30-42. Additional supplements appear in the following issues of *English Literature in Transition:* IV, No. 3 (1961), 52-53; V, No. 1 (1962), 45-46; V, No. 4 (1962), 33-35; VI, No. 1(1963), 52-53; VI, No. 2 (1963), 117-118; VI, No. 3 (1963), 167-169; VI, No. 4 (1963), 237; VII, No. 1 (1964), 32-33; VII, No. 2 (1964), 120-121; VIII, No. 2 (1965), 122-123; VIII, No. 5 (1965), 301-302; IX, No. 4 (1966), 225-228; XI, No. 1 (1968), 50-54; XII, No. 1 (1969), 45-48; XIV, No. 1 (1971), 75-83; XV, No. 1 (1972), 85-90; XVI, No. 2 (1973), 154-161; and XVII, No. 1 (1974), 49-53.

CRITICISM ABOUT

Dunleavy, Janet. *George Moore: The Artist's Vision, the Storyteller's Art.* Lewisburg, Pa.: Bucknell University, 1973.

Richard Murphy (1927-   )

POETRY

The Archaeology of Love: Poems. Glenageary: Dolmen, 1955.

The Battle of Aughrim and The God Who Eats the Corn. London: Faber and Faber; New York: Knopf, 1968.

High Island: New and Selected Poems. London: Faber and Faber; New York: Harper and Row, 1974.

The Last Galway Hooker. Dublin: Dolmen, 1961. 500 copies with 50 numbered and signed.

Sailing to an Island: A poem. Dublin: Pvt. ptd. at the Dolmen, 1955. 35 numbered copies.

Sailing to an Island: Poems. London: Faber and Faber; New York: Chilmark, 1963.

The Woman of the House: An Elegy. Dublin: Dolmen, 1959. 275 copies with 25 numbered.

JOINT AUTHOR

With Jon Silkin and Nathaniel Tarn. *Penguin Modern Poets, 7.* Harmondsworth: Penguin, 1965.

Three Irish Poets: John Montague, Thomas Kinsella, Richard Murphy. A poetry reading presented by the Dolmen Press at the Royal Hibernian Hotel, Dublin, Feb. 3, 1961. Dublin: Dolmen, 1961. 250 copies.

T. C. Murray (1873-1959)

COLLECTED AND SELECTED PLAYS

Maurice Harte and A Stag at Bay. London: Allen and Unwin, 1934.

Spring; and other plays. Dublin: Talbot, 1917. London: Allen and Unwin, 1926.

The Pipe in the Field and Birthright. London: Allen and Unwin, 1928.

INDIVIDUAL PLAYS

Aftermath: A play in three acts. Dublin: Talbot; London: Unwin, 1922.

Autumn Fire: A play in three acts. London: Allen and Unwin, 1925. Boston and New York: Houghton Mifflin, 1926.

Birthright: A play in two acts. Dublin: Maunsel, 1911.

Maurice Harte: A play in two acts. Dublin and London: Maunsel, 1912.

Michaelmas Eve: A play in three acts. London: Allen and Unwin, 1932.

Spring: A play in one act. Dublin: Duffy, 1956.

NOVEL

Spring Horizon: A novel. New York: Nelson, 1937.

FOREWORD

Plunkett, Grace. *Doctors Recommend It: An Abbey Theatre Tonic in 12 doses.* Dublin: Ptd. for subscribers only by Colm Ó Lochlainn at the Sign of the Three Candles, 1930. Not more than 500 copies ptd. for subscribers.

Sean O'Casey, pseud. of John Casey (1880-1963)

COLLECTED AND SELECTED WORKS

Autobiographies. London: Macmillan, 1963.

Behind the Green Curtains, Figure in the Night, The Moon Shines on Kylenamoe: Three Plays. London: Macmillan; New York: St. Martin's, 1961.

Blasts and Benedictions. Ed. with intro. by Ronald Ayling. London: Macmillan; New York: St. Martin's, 1967.

The Collected Plays of Sean O'Casey. London: Macmillan, 1949–. Vol. 1, 1949. Vol. 2, 1949. Vol. 3, 1951. Vol. 4, 1951. New York: St. Martin's, 1957.

Feathers from the Green Crow. Ed. Robert Hogan. Columbia: University of Missouri, 1962.

Five Irish Plays. London: Macmillan, 1935.

Five One Act Plays. New York: St. Martin's, 1958.

Juno and the Paycock and The Plough and the Stars. London: Macmillan, 1948. New York: St. Martin's, 1957.

Mirror in My House: The autobiographies of Sean O'Casey. New York: Macmillan, 1956.

The Sean O'Casey Reader: Plays, Autobiographies, Opinions. Ed. with an intro. by Brooks Atkinson. London: Macmillan; New York: St. Martin's, 1968.

Selected Plays of Sean O'Casey. Sel. with fore. by O'Casey. Intro. by John Gassner. London: Braziller, 1954.

Three More Plays. Intro. by J. C. Trewin. London: Macmillan; New York: St. Martin's, 1965.

Three Plays. New York: St. Martin's, 1961. London: Macmillan, 1964.

Two Plays. New York: Macmillan, 1925. London: Macmillan, 1930.

Windfalls: Stories, Poems, and Plays. London and New York: Macmillan, 1930.

INDIVIDUAL PLAYS

The Bishop's Bonfire: A sad play written to the tune of a polka. London and New York: Macmillan; New York: St. Martin's, 1955.

Cock-a-Doodle Dandy. London and New York: Macmillan, 1949.

The Drums of Father Ned: A microcosm of Ireland. London and Toronto: Macmillan; New York: St. Martin's, 1960.

Juno and the Paycock: A tragedy in three acts. London and New York: French, 1932.

Oak Leaves and Lavender; or, a world on wallpaper. London and New York: Macmillan, 1946. New York: Macmillan, 1947.

The Plough and the Stars: A tragedy in four acts. London: Macmillan, 1926. London and New York: French, 1932.

Purple Dust: A wayward comedy in three acts. London and Toronto: Macmillan, 1940. New York: Macmillan, 1941.

Red Roses for Me: A play in four acts. London: Macmillan, 1942. New York and Toronto: Macmillan, 1943.

The Shadow of a Gunman: A tragedy in two acts. New York and London: French; 1932.

The Silver Tassie: A tragicomedy in four acts. London and New York: Macmillan, 1928.

The Star Turns Red: A play. London and Toronto: Macmillan, 1940.

Within the Gates: A play in four scenes in a London park. Music by Herbert Hughes. London: Macmillan, 1933. New York and Toronto: Macmillan, 1934.

AUTOBIOGRAPHIES AND CRITICISM

Drums Under the Window: Autobiographical reminiscences. London: Macmillan, 1945. New York: Macmillan, 1946.

The Flying Wasp: A laughing look-over of what has been said about the things of the theatre by the English dramatic critics, with many merry and delicious comments thereon, with some shrewd remarks by the author on the wise, delicious, and dignified tendencies in the theatre of to-day. London and New York: Macmillan, 1937.

Green Crow. New York: Braziller, 1956. London: Allen, 1957.

I Knock at the Door: Swift Glances at the things that made me. London and New York: Macmillan, 1939. New York: Macmillan, 1940.

Inishfallen Fare Thee Well. London and New York: Macmillan, 1949.

Pictures in the Hallway. London and New York: Macmillan, 1942.

Rose and Crown. London and New York: Macmillan, 1952.

The Sting and the Twinkle: Conversations. Edited by E. H. Mikhail and John O'Riordan. New York: Barnes & Noble, 1974.

Sunset and Evening Star. New York and London: Macmillan, 1954.

Under a Colored Cap. London: Macmillan; New York: St. Martin's, 1963.

UNDER THE PSEUDONYM OF SEAN O'CATHOSAIGH

POETRY

England's Conscription Appeal to the Irish Dead. Air—"Harp and Lion." n.p., n.d.

More Wren Songs. [Dublin: O'Connor, 1918].

Songs of the Wren: Humorous and sentimental. To well known airs. Dublin: O'Connor [1918].

PROSE

The Story of the Irish Citizen Army. Pref. Dublin and London: Maunsel, 1919.

The Story of Thomas Ashe. Fore. Dublin: O'Connor, 1917. Enl. ed. with title *The Sacrifice of Thomas Ashe.* Fore. and Lament for Thomas Ashe. Dublin: O'Connor, 1918.

LETTERS

Two Letters by Sean O'Casey referring to the assassination of President Kennedy. From the correspondence of Sean O'Casey and Franklin D. Murphy, 1963 [n.p.] Privately printed, 1966.

Krause, David. *Sean O'Casey's Letters: Self-Portrait of the Artist as a Man.* Dublin: Dolmen Press; Chester Springs, Pa.: Dufour, 1968.

FOREWORD

Gregory, Isabella Augusta. *Selected Plays.* Chosen and with an intro. by Elizabeth Coxhead. London and New York: Putnam, 1962.

CRITICAL AND BIOGRAPHICAL STUDIES

Armstrong, William A. *Sean O'Casey.* London: Pub. for the British Council and the National Book League by Longmans, Green, 1965. Writers and Their Work, No. 198.

Ayling, Ronald, editor. *Sean O'Casey.* London: Macmillan, 1969. Nashville: Aurora, 1970.

Benstock, Bernard. *Sean O'Casey* (Irish Writers Series). Lewisburg: Bucknell University, 1971.

Cowasjee, Saros. *Sean O'Casey: The man behind the masks.* Fore. by Eileen O'Casey. Edinburgh and London: Oliver and Boyd, 1963. New York: St. Martin's, c1963, 1964.

———. *O'Casey.* London: Oliver and Boyd, 1966. New York: Barnes and Noble, 1967.

Fallon, Gabriel. *Sean O'Casey: The Man I Knew.* London: Routledge and Kegan Paul; Boston and Toronto: Little, Brown, 1965.

Hogan, Robert. *The Experiments of Sean O'Casey.* New York: St. Martin's, 1960.

Koslow, Jules. *The Green and the Red.* New York: Arts, 1950.

——. *Sean O'Casey: The Man and His Plays.* New York: Citadel, 1966. London: MacGibbon & Kee, 1967.

Krause, David. *Sean O'Casey. The man and his work.* London: MacGibbon and Kee; New York: Macmillan, 1960.

Malone, Maureen. *Plays of Sean O'Casey.* Carbondale: University of Southern Illinois; London & Amsterdam: Feffer and Simons, 1969.

McCann, Sean. *The World of Sean O'Casey.* London: New English Library; New York: Twayne, 1966.

Marguilies, Martin B. *The Early Life of Sean O'Casey.* Dublin: Dolmen; New York: Humanities, 1971.

Mikhail, E. H. *Sean O'Casey: A Bibliography of Criticism.* Seattle: University of Washington; London: Macmillan, 1972.

O'Casey, Eileen R. (Mrs. Sean). *Sean.* London: Macmillan, 1971. New York: Coward, McCann and Geoghegan, 1972.

Wittig, Kurt. *Sean O'Casey als Dramatiker.* Ein Beitag zum Nachkriegsdrama Irlands. Inaaugural Dissertation zur Erlangung der Doktor würde der Honen Philosophischen Fakultät der Martin Luther–Universitüt Halle–Wittenburg. Wittenberg: Halle, 1937. Leipzig: Scharf [1937].

Frank O'Connor, pseud. of Michael O'Donovan (1903-1966)

COLLECTED AND SELECTED STORIES

Bones of Contention; and other stories. London, New York, and Toronto: Macmillan, 1936.

Collection Three. London: Macmillan; Dublin: Gill and Macmillan, 1969.

Collection Two. Intro. London: Macmillan, 1964.

Common Cord: Stories and tales. London: Macmillan, 1947. New York: Knopf, 1948.

Crab Apple Jelly: Stories and tales. London: Macmillan; New York: Knopf, 1944.

Domestic Relations: Short Stories. London: Hamilton; New York: Knopf, 1957.

Fish for Friday and Other Stories. London: Pan, 1971.

Guests of the Nation. London: Macmillan; New York: Macmillan, 1931.

More Stories. New York: Knopf, 1954.

My Oedipus Complex; and other stories. Harmondsworth: Penguin Books in association with Hamilton, 1963.

Selected Stories. Dublin and London: Fridberg, 1946.

A Set of Variations. 27 stories. New York: Knopf, 1969. (Dist. by Random House.)

Stories by Frank O'Connor. New York: Vintage, 1956.

Stories of Frank O'Connor. New York: Knopf, 1952. London: Hamilton, 1953.

Three Tales. Dublin: Cuala, 1941.

Traveller's Samples: Stories and tales. London and Toronto: Macmillan; New York: Knopf, 1951.

NOVELS

Dutch Interior. London: Macmillan; New York: Knopf, 1940.

The Saint and Mary Kate. London and New York: Macmillan, 1932.

AUTOBIOGRAPHY

My Father's Son. London: Macmillan; New York: Knopf, 1968.

An Only Child. London: Macmillan; New York: Knopf, 1961.

POEMS AND TRANSLATIONS

The Fountain of Magic. Trans. from the Irish. Pref. London: Macmillan, 1939.

Kings, Lords, and Commons: An anthology from the Irish. Pref. New York: Knopf, 1959. London: Macmillan, 1961.

A Lament for Art O'Leary. Trans. from the Irish. Pref. Dublin: Cuala, 1940. 130 numbered copies.

Little Monasteries. Dublin: Dolmen, 1963.

Lords and Commons. Trans. from the Irish. Dublin: Cuala, 1938.

The Midnight Court: A rhythmical Lacchanalia from the Irish of Bryon Merryman. Dublin and London: Fridberg, 1945.

Three Old Brothers; and other poems. London: Nelson, 1936.

Wild Bird's Nest: Poems from the Irish. With an essay on the character in Irish literature by AE. Dublin: Cuala, 1932. 250 copies.

CRITICISM AND BIOGRAPHY BY

Art of the Theatre. Dublin and London: Fridberg, 1947.

The Backward Look: A Survey of Irish Literature. London: Macmillan, 1967. Pub. in the U.S.A. with title *A Short History of Irish Literature: A Backward Look.* New York: Putnam's, 1967.

The Bigfellow. A life of Michael Collins. London: Nelson, 1937. Same with title *The Big Fellow. Michael Collins and the Irish Revolution.* Fore. Dublin: Clonmore and Reynolds; London: Burns and Oates, 1966. Pub. in the U.S.A. with title *Death in Dublin. Michael Collins and Irish Revolution.* Garden City, New York: Doubleday, 1937.

Irish Miles. London: Macmillan, 1947.

Leinster, Munster, and Connaught. London: Hale; New York: Macmillan [1950].

Lonely Voice: A study of the short story. London: Macmillan; Cleveland: World Publishing Co., 1963.

Mirror in the Roadway: A study of the modern novel. Intro. New York: Knopf, 1956. London: Hamilton, 1957.

A Picture Book. Dublin: Cuala, 1943.

The Road to Stratford. London: Methuen, 1948. New and rev. ed. called the American version with title *Shakespeare's Progress.* Cleveland and New York: World Publishing Co., 1960.

Towards an Appreciation of Literature. Dublin: Metropolitan, 1945.

JOINT AUTHOR

With Michael Aldenhoff. *Die Amerikanerin: Ihre Macht und ihre Moral.* Dusseldorf: Hellas-Verlag, 1958.

EDITED BY

A Book of Ireland. London and Glasgow: Collins, 1959.

A Golden Treasury of Irish Poetry: A.D. 600-1200. Edited and translated with Greene, David Herbert. London: Macmillan, 1967.

Modern Irish Short Stories. Sel. with an intro. London: Oxford, 1957.

INTRODUCTION

Cross, Eric. *The Tailor and Ansty*. Intro. London: Chapman and Hall, 1942.

Dafydd ap Gwilym: Selected Poems. Trans. by Nigel Heseltine. Pref. Dublin: Cuala, 1944. 280 numbered copies with 250 for sale.

O'Lochalainn, Colm (ed. and coll.). *Irish Street Ballads*. Appreciation. New York: Citadel, 1960.

BIOGRAPHICAL AND CRITICAL STUDIES

Matthews, James. *Frank O'Connor*. (Irish Writers Series). Lewisburg: Bucknell University (in prep.).

Sheehy, Michael, editor. *Michael/Franks Studies on Frank O'Connor*. London: Macmillan; Dublin: Gill-Macmillan; New York: Knopf, 1969.

Eimar O'Duffy (1893-1935)

NOVELS

Asses in Clover. London and New York: Putnam, 1933.

The Bird Cage: A mystery novel. London: Bles, 1932.

Head of a Girl. London: Bles, 1935.

King Goshawk and the Birds. London, New York, and Toronto: Macmillan, 1926.

The Lion and the Fox. Dublin: Lester [1921].

Miss Rudd and Some Lovers. Dublin: Talbot; London: Unwin, 1923.

Printer's Errors. Dublin: Lester; London: Parson [1920].

The Secret Enemy. London: Bles, 1933.

The Spacious Adventures of the Man in the Street. Fore. London: Macmillan, 1928.

The Wasted Island. Dublin: Lester [1919]. London: Macmillan, 1929.

PLAYS

Bricriu's Feast: A comedy in three acts with an epilogue. Dublin: Lester [1919].

*The Phoenix on the Roof. 1923.

The Walls of Athens: A comedy in allegory. Dublin: The Irish Review, 1914.

POETRY

A Lay of the Liffey. Dublin: Candle, 1918.

National Christmas. London: Lahr, 1931. 100 signed copies.

CRITICISM

Consumer Credit. Fore. by the Most Hon. the Marquis of Tavistock. London: Prosperity League [1934].

Life and Money. Economics and a practical scheme for remedying the present industrial and financial chaos. Intro. London and New York: Putnam, 1932. New ed. with title *Life and Money*. Being a critical examination of the principles and practice of orthodox economics with a practical scheme to end the muddle it has made of our civilization. London and New York: Putnam, 1933. New ed. with title *Life and Money*. Being a critical examination of the principles and practice of orthodox economics with a practical scheme to end the muddle it has made of our civilization with an outline of principles and proposals of social credit. London: Putnam, 1935.

EDITED BY

A College Chorus. A collection of humorous verses by students of University College, Dublin, from the pages of "St. Stephen's" and "The National Student." Dublin: Lester [1920].

The National Student: A magazine of university life. Vol. V, No. 3 (May, 1915). [Dublin.]

BIBLIOGRAPHICAL, BIOGRAPHICAL AND
CRITICAL STUDIES ABOUT

Hogan, Robert G. *Eimar O'Duffy*. (Irish Writers Series). Lewisburg:
Bucknell University, 1972.

Sean O'Faolain (1900-   )

FICTION AND PLAYS

Bird Alone. London: Cape; New York: Viking, 1936.

The Born Genius: A short story. Detroit: Schuman's, 1936. 250 copies.

Come Back to Erin: A novel. London: Cape; New York: Viking, 1940.

Finest Short Stories of Sean O'Faolain. Boston and Toronto: Little,
Brown; New York: Bantam, 1957.

The Heat of the Sun: Stories and other tales. London: Hart-Davis; Boston and Toronto: Little, Brown, 1966.

I Remember! I Remember! Boston and Toronto: Little, Brown, 1961.
London: Hart-Davis, 1962.

The Man Who Invented Sin; and other stories. New York: Devin-Adair,
1948.

Midsummer Night Madness; and other stories. Intro. by Edward Gar-
nett. London and Toronto: Cape; New York: Viking, 1932.

A Nest of Simple Folk: A novel. London: Cape, 1933. New York: Viking, 1934.

A Purse of Coppers: Short stories. London and Toronto: Cape, 1937.
New York: Viking, 1938.

She Had to Do Something: A comedy in three acts. London: Cape,
1938.

Stories. London: Hart-Davis, c1957, 1958.

Stories of Sean O'Faolain. Harmondsworth: Penguin, 1970.

The Talking Trees and Other Stories. Boston: Little, Brown, 1970;
London: Jonathan Cape, 1971.

Teresa; and other stories. London: Cape, 1947.

There's a Birdie in the Cage. London: Grayson and Grayson, 1935. 285 numbered and signed copies with 250 for sale.

BIOGRAPHIES BY

Constance Markievicz; or, the average revolutionary. A biography. London and Toronto: Cape, 1934. Rev. ed., London: Sphere Books, 1968.

De Valera: A new biography written specially for this series. Harmondsworth: Penguin, 1939.

The Great O'Neill: A biography of Hugh O'Neill, Earl of Tyron, 1550-1616. London: Longmans, Green; New York: Duell, Sloan, Pearce, 1942.

King of the Beggars: A life of Daniel O'Connell, the Irish liberator, in a study of the rise of the modern Irish democracy (1775-1847). London: Edinburgh, Paris, Melbourne, and Toronto: Nelson; New York: Viking, 1938. Abr. ed., Dublin: Parkside [1945].

The Life Story of Eamon De Valera. Dublin and Cork: Talbot, 1933.

Newman's Way. London, New York, and Toronto: Longmans, Green, 1952. Pub. in the U.S.A. with title *Newman's Way. The odyssey of John Henry Newman.* New York: Devin-Adair, 1952.

TRAVEL

Autumn in Italy. See *South To Sicily.*

The Irish. Pref. West Drayton: Penguin, 1947.

The Irish: A character study. New York: Devin-Adair, 1949.

The Irish. Revised edition. Harmondsworth: Penguin, 1969.

An Irish Journey. London, New York, and Toronto: Longmans, Green, 1940.

South to Sicily. London: Collins, 1953. Pub. in the USA with the title *Autumn in Italy.* New York: Devin-Adair, 1953.

The Story of Ireland. London: Collins; New York and Los Angeles: Hastings House, 1943.

A Summer in Italy. London: Eyre and Spottiswoode, 1949. New York: Devin-Adair, 1950.

AUTOBIOGRAPHY

Vive Moi! Boston and Toronto: Little, Brown, c1963, 1964. London: Hart-Davis, 1965.

CRITICISM

Short Stories: A study in pleasure. Boston: Little, Brown, 1961.

The Short Story. London and Toronto: Collins, 1948. New York: Devin-Adair, 1951.

The Vanishing Hero: Studies in the novelists of the twenties. London: Eyre and Spottiswoode, 1956. Boston and Toronto: Little, Brown, 1957.

"With the Gaels of Wexford." Reamh-Radh. Enniscorthy: Ptd. at the Echo Offices and Pub. by Sean O'Faolain, 1955.

EDITED BY

The Bell. Vol. I-XI. Jan. 1940 to Dec. 1946. Cont. until 1954, Vol. XIX, with Paedar O'Donnell as editor.

Eighty-three Thousand Two Hundred and Twenty-Two. I did Penal Servitude. Pref. Dublin: Metropolitan, 1945.

Lover, Samuel. *Adventures of Handy Andy.* Ed. with a fore. Dublin: Parkside [1945].

Moore, Tom. *Lyrics and Satires from Tom Moore.* Dublin: Cuala, 1929. 130 copies.

Schnack, Elisabeth. *Irische Erzähler: Auswahl und Ubertragüng.* Fore. Zurich: Manesse, 1952.

The Silver Branch. A collection of the best old Irish Lyrics, variously trans. London: Cape; New York: Macmillan, 1938.

Tone, Wolfe Theobald. *The Autobiography of Wolfe Theobald Tone.* Abg. and ed. London: Nelson, 1937.

CRITICAL STUDIES

Browne, Joseph. *Sean O'Faolain.* (Irish Writers Series). Lewisburg: Bucknell University [n. d.].

Doyle, Paul A. *Sean O'Faolain.* New York: Twayne, 1968.

Harmon, Maurice. *Sean O'Faolain.* Notre Dame: Notre Dame University, 1967.

Roibeard Ó Farachain, pseud. of
Robert Farren (1909-   )

POETRY

The First Exile. A Poem. See *This Man Was Ireland.*

Rime, Gentlemen, Please: Poems. London and New York: Sheed and Ward, 1945.

Selected Poems. London and New York: Sheed and Ward, 1951.

This Man Was Ireland: A Poem. New York: Sheed and Ward, 1943. Pub. in England with the title *The First Exile. A Poem.* London: Sheed and Ward, 1944.

Thronging Feet: Poems. Intro. by Daniel Corkery. London and New York: Sheed and Ward, 1936.

Time's Wall Asunder: Poems. London and New York: Sheed and Ward, 1939.

PROSE

The Course of Irish Verse. London: Sheed and Ward, 1948.

Fíon gan Mhoirt: cnuasach géarr-scéalta. Baile Átha Cliath: Oifig an tSoláthair, 1938.

How to Enjoy Poetry. New York: Sheed and Ward, 1948.

Towards an Appreciation of Poetry. Dublin: Metropolitan, 1947.

EDITED BY

Éire: Bliainiris Ghaedheal rogha saothair Gaedeal mheó. Baile Átha Cliath: Muinnts Cathail, 1940. Continued without Ó Farachain.

INTRODUCTION

Faller, Kevin. *Lyric and Script.* Dublin, London, and Paris: Loescher [1947].

TRANSLATED BY

Barry, Dermot. *Tomás Ó Créagáin.* Baile Áthe Cliath: Oifig an tSoláthair, 1954.

McManus, Francis. *Tóirthneach luimighe: Dráma staireamhial i dtrí radharcanna*. Baile Átha Cliath: Brún agus 0 Nullain [1935].

Liam O'Flaherty (1897-   )

BIBLIOGRAPHY

Doyle, Paul A. *Liam O'Flaherty: An Annotated Bibliography*. Troy, New York: Whitston Publishing Co., 1972.

COLLECTIONS OF SHORT STORIES

Dúil. Baile Átha Cliath: Sáirséal agus Dill, 1953.

The Fairy Goose; and two other stories. New York: Gaige, dist. by Random House; London: Faber and Faber, 1927. 190 signed copies, 12 on green paper, signed and with a note.

Irish Portraits: 14 Short Stories. London: Sphere, 1970.

The Mountain Tavern; and other stories. London: Cape; New York: Harcourt, Brace, 1929.

More Short Stories of Liam O'Flaherty. London: New English Library, 1971.

Red Barbara; and other stories. New York; Gaige, dist. by Random House; London: Faber and Gwyer, 1928.

Selected Short Stories. London: New English Library, 1970.

The Short Stories of Liam O'Flaherty. London :Cape, 1937.

The Short Stories of Liam O'Flaherty. London: Brown, Watson, 1961.

The Short Stories of Liam O'Flaherty. Abridged ed. London: New English Library, 1970.

Spring Sowing. London: Cape, 1924. New York: Cape and Smith, 1929.

Stories of Liam O'Flaherty. Sel. with an intro. by Vivian Mercier. New York: Devin-Adair, 1956.

The Tent. London: Cape, 1926.

Two Lovely Beasts; and other stories. London: Gollancz, 1948. New York: Devin-Adair, 1950.

The Wild Swan; and other stories. Fore. by Rhys Davies. London: Jackson, 1932. 550 numbered and signed copies.

The Wounded Cormorant and Other Stories. Intro. by Vivian Mercier. New York: Norton, 1973. ("A selection of stories from the Stories of L. Ó F." [c1956].)

NOVELS AND PLAYS

The Assassin. London: Cape, 1928. 150 numbered and signed copies and unlimited ed. New York: Harcourt, 1928.

The Black Soul. London: Cape, 1924. New York: Boni and Liveright [1924].

The Child of God. London: Archer, 1926. 100 copies, 25 with a portrait by William Roberts.

Civil War. London: Archer, 1925. 100 numbered and signed copies.

Darkness: A tragedy in three acts. London: Archer, 1926. 100 numbered and signed copies.

Ecstasy of Angus. London: Joiner and Steele, 1931. 365 numbered and signed copies.

Famine. London: Gollancz; New York: Random House; New York: The Literary Guild, 1937.

Hollywood Cemetery. London: Gollancz, 1935.

House of Gold. London: Cape; New York: Harcourt, 1929.

The Informer. London: Cape; New York: Knopf, 1925. Same with afterword by Donagh MacDonagh. New York: New American Library, 1961.

Insurrection. London: Gollancz; New York: Longmans, Green, 1950.

Land. New York and Toronto: Random House; London: Gollancz, 1946.

The Martyr. London: Gollancz; New York: Macmillan, 1933.

Mr. Gilhooley. London: Cape, 1926. New York: Harcourt, 1927. Rev. ed. by Cape in 1927.

The Puritan. London: Cape, 1932. New York: Harcourt [1932].

Return of the Brute. London: Mandrake, 1929. New York: Harcourt, 1930.

Shame the Devil. London: Grayson and Grayson, 1934. 100 copies each with a page of the MS and unlimited ed.

Skerrett. London: Gollancz; New York: Long and Smith, 1932.

The Terrorist. London: Archer, 1926. 100 numbered and signed copies.

Thy Neighbor's Wife. London: Cape, 1923. New York: Boni and Liveright, 1924.

CRITICAL AND HISTORICAL STUDIES

A Cure for Unemployment. London: Lahr, 1931. 100 numbered and signed copies and unlimited ed.

I Went to Russia. London: Cape; New York: Harcourt, 1931.

Joseph Conrad. An appreciation. London: Lahr [1930].

The Life of Tim Healy. London: Cape; New York: Harcourt, 1927.

My Experiences (1896-1923). n.p., n.d.

A Tourist's Guide to Ireland. London: Mandrake [1929].

Two Years. London and Toronto: Cape; New York: Harcourt, 1930.

INTRODUCTION BY

Lowe, Alfred. *Six Cartoons*. Intro. London: Foyle, 1930. 750 numbered copies.

Davies, Rhys. *The Stars, The World, and The Women*. London: Jackson, 1930.

BIOGRAPHICAL AND CRITICAL STUDIES

Doyle, Paul A. *Liam O'Flaherty*. New York: Twayne, 1971.

O'Brien, James. *Liam O'Flaherty*. (Irish Writers Series). Lewisburg: Bucknell University, 1973.

Sheeran, Patrick F. *Novels of Liam O'Flaherty: A Study in Romantic Realism*. New York: Barnes & Noble, 1973.

Zneimer, John Nicholas. *The Literary Vision of Liam O'Flaherty*. Syracuse: Syracuse University, 1970.

Standish James O'Grady (1846-1928)

COLLECTED AND SELECTED WORKS

The Cuchulain Cycle. 3 vols. Vol. 1. *The Coming of Cuchulain.* Pref. and intro. by AE. Dublin: Talbot [1938]. Vol .2. *In the Gates of the North.* Intro. Dublin and Cork: Talbot [1938]. Vol. 3. *The Triumph and Passing of Cuchulain.* Dublin: Talbot [1938]. These books are identical to the issue Dublin: Talbot; London: Unwin [1920]. 3 vols. which appeared without the appellation *The Cuchulain Cycle.*

Selected Essays and Passages. Intro. by Ernest A. Boyd. Dublin: Talbot; London: Unwin [1917]. New York: Stokes [1918].

FICTION

The Bog of the Stars; and other stories and sketches of Elizabethan Ireland. Dublin: Sealy, Bryers, and Walker; London: Unwin; New York: Kenedy, 1893.

The Chain of Gold; or, in crannied rocks. A boy's tale of adventure on the wild west coast of Ireland. London: Unwin, 1895. Dublin: Talbot [1921].

The Coming of Cuchulain: A romance of the heroic age in Ireland. Pref. London: Methuen, 1894. See *The Cuchulain Cycle.*

The Departure of Dermot. Dublin: Talbot, 1917.

Finn and His Companions. Pref. London: Unwin, 1892. New ed. bound with *The Masque of Finn.* Pref. and notes. Dublin: Talbot; London: Unwin, 1921.

Fionn and His Companions. Illus. by Brid Ni Rinn. Dublin: Talbot, 1970. "Present edition . . . intended for the reading of young people, has been shortened by omission of the original preface . . . and *The Masque of Fionn.*" Pub. in 1921 under the title: *Finn and his Companions.*

The Flight of the Eagle. Pref. London: Lawrence and Bullen, 1897. Same with pref. Dublin: Talbot; London: Unwin [1921].

Hugh Roe O'Donnell: A sixteenth-century Irish historical play. Written to be performed in the woods of Shustown, in the county of Kilkenny by the Neophytes. Belfast: Nelson and Knox, 1902.

In the Gates of the North. Intro. Kilkenny: O'Grady, 1901. See *The Cuchulain Cycle.*

In the Wake of the King James; or, Dun-Randal on the Sea. London: Dent, 1896.

Lost on Du Corrig; or, Twixt Earth and Ocean. London, Paris, Melbourne: Cassell, 1894. Same with pref. Dublin: Talbot; London: Unwin [1921].

The Masque of Finn. Kilkenny: O'Grady, 1907. See *Finn and his Companions.*

Red Hugh's Captivity. A picture of Ireland, social and political, in the reign of Queen Elizabeth. Intro. London: Ward and Downey, 1889.

The Triumph and Passing of Cuchulain. Dublin: Talbot; London: Unwin, New York: Stokes, 1920. See *The Cuchulain Cycle.*

Ulick the Ready. A romance of Elizabethan Ireland. Pref. New York: Dodd, Mead; London: Downey, 1896. Same with title *Ulick the Ready; or, The chieftain's last rally.* Dublin: Talbot; London: Unwin [1920].

NON-FICTION

All Ireland. Pref. Dublin: Sealy, Bryers, and Walker; London: Unwin, 1898.

Early Bardic Literature. London: Low, Searle, Marston, Rivington, 1879.

History of Ireland. Intros. 2 vols. Vol. 1. *The Heroic Period.* Dublin: Ponsonby; London: Low, Searle, Marston, Rivington [1878]. Vol. 2. *Cuchulain and His Contemporaries.* Intro. is *Early Bardic Ireland.* Dublin: Ponsonby; London: Low, Searle, Marston, Rivington, 1880.

History of Ireland: Critical and Philosophical. Vol. 1. Dublin: Ponsonby; London: Low, Searle, Marston, Rivington, 1881.

The Story of Ireland. London: Methuen, 1893.

Toryism and the Tory Democrat. Pref. London: Chapman and Hall, 1886.

UNDER THE PSEUDONYM OF LUKE NETTERVILLE

The Queen of the World; or, Under the Tyranny. Intro. London: Lawrence and Bullen, 1900.

EDITED BY

Carew, George, Earle of Totnes. *Pacata Hibernia; or, a history of the wars in Ireland during the reign of Queen Elizabeth especially written within the province of Munster under the government of Sir George Carew and compiled by his jurisdiction and appointment.* Ed. with intro. and notes. 2 vols. London: Downey, 1896.

Ferguson, Sir Samuel. *Poems of Sir Samuel Ferguson.* New York: Stokes, 1918.

**The Kilkenny Moderator.* Kilkenny, 1898-1901.

Todhunter, John. *Essays.* Fore. London: Mathews, 1920.

EDITED UNDER THE PSEUDONYM OF ARTHUR CLIVE

Shelley, Percy Bysshe. *Scintilla Shelleiana: Shelley's attitude towards religion, explained and defended by himself.* Ed. with pref. Dublin: McGee, 1875.

CRITICAL AND BIOGRAPHICAL STUDIES

Marcus, Phillip L. *Standish O'Grady.* (Irish Writers Series). Lewisburg: Bucknell University, 1970.

O'Grady, Hugh Art. *Standish James O'Grady: The man and the writer.* A memoir by his son Hugh Art O'Grady, Litt.D., with a fore. by A. P. Graves and contributions by AE and others. Dublin and Cork: Talbot, 1929.

O'Hegarty, Patrick Sarsfield. *A Bibliography of Books Written by Standish O'Grady.* Dublin: Pvt. ptd. by Thom. 1930.

Seumas O'Kelly (1881-1918)

PLAYS

The Bribe: A play in three acts. Dublin and London: Maunsel, 1914.

The Golden Barque and The Weaver's Grave. Dublin: Talbot; London: Unwin; New York: Putnam, 1919.

The Matchmakers: A comedy in one act. Dublin: Gill, 1908.

Meadowsweet: A comedy in one act. n.p. [1919]. Dublin: Talbot [1925].

The Shuiler's Child: A tragedy in two acts. Dublin: Maunsel, 1909.

Three Plays. Dublin: Gill, 1912.

FICTION

By the Stream of Killmeen. Dublin: Sealy, Bryers, and Walker, 1906.

Hillsiders. Dublin: Talbot; London: Unwin, 1921.

Irish Short Stories. Cork: Mercier [1966].

The Lady of Deerpark. London: Methuen, 1917. Abr. ed., London: Mellifont, 1944.

A Land of Loneliness and Other Stories. Sel. with critical intro. by Eamon Grennan. Dublin: Gill and Macmillan, 1969.

The Leprechaun of Killmeen. Dublin: Lester [1920].

The Marriage Money and An Island Eve. Dublin: Catholic Truth Society of Ireland [1928].

The Parnellite. Naas: The Leinster Leader [1919].

The Revenge of Seaghan Buidhe. Dublin: Catholic Truth Society of Ireland [1928].

Waysiders: Stories of Connacht. Dublin: Talbot; London: Unwin, 1917. New York: Stokes, 1918.

The Weaver's Grave. Dublin: Talbot [1922].

Wet Clay. Dublin: Talbot; London: Unwin, 1922. New York: Stokes, 1923.

POETRY

Ranns and Ballads. Dublin: Candle, 1918.

EDITED BY

*The Dublin Saturday Post.

*The Leinster Leader. Naas, 1903-12.

*Nationality. Dublin, May to November, 1918.

*The Southern Star. Skibbereen, 1903.

BIBLIOGRAPHY

O'Hegarty, Patrick Sarsfield. *A Bibliography of the Books by Seumas O'Kelly*. Dublin: Thom, 1934.

BIOGRAPHY AND CRITICISM

Saul, G. B. *Seumas O'Kelly*. (Irish Writers Series). Lewisburg, Pa.: Bucknell University, 1971.

Brian O'Nolan (1912-1965)

UNDER THE PSEUDONYM OF FLANN O'BRIEN

At Swim-two-birds. London and New York: Longmans, Green; New York: Pantheon, 1939.

The Dalkey Archive. London: MacGibbon and Kee, 1964. New York: Macmillan, c1964, 1965.

Stories and Plays by Flann O'Brien. London: Hart-Davis MacGibbon, 1973.

The Hard Life. An exegesis of squalor. London: MacGibbon and Kee, 1961. New York: Pantheaon, c1961, 1962.

The Third Policeman. London: MacGibbon and Kee, 1967.

UNDER THE PSEUDONYM OF MYLES na GOPALEEN

An Beál Bocht nó an milleánach: Droch-sgéal ar an droch-shaoghal curtha i n-eagar le Myles na gCopaleen. Intro. Baile Átha Cliath: An Press Náisiunta [1941]. Same with an additional intro. by the editor. Baile Átha Cliant: Dolmen, 1964.

The Best of Myles: A selection from 'Cruiskeen Lawn.' Ed. with a pref. by Kevin O Nolan. New York: Walker, 1968.

Cruiskeen Lawn. Dublin: Cahill [1943].

Faustus Kelly: A play in three acts. Dublin: Cahill, 1943.

The Poor Mouth (An Beal Bocht): A Bad Story About A Hard Life. Edited by Myles na Gopaleen. Translated by Patrick C. Power. Illustrated by Ralph Steadman. London: Hart-Davis-MacGibbon, 1973. New York: Viking, 1974.

BIOGRAPHICAL AND CRITICAL STUDIES ABOUT

Benstock, Bernard. *Flann O'Brien*. (Irish Writers Series). Lewisburg, Pa.: Bucknell University [n. d.]

O'Keefe, Timothy, editor. *Myles: Portraits of Brian O'Nolan*. London: Martin Brian & O'Keefe, 1973.

Conal Holmes O'Connell O'Riordan, pseud. of F. Norreys Connell (1874-1948)

PLAYS

Captain Falstaff; and other plays. London: Arrowsmith, 1935.

His Majesty's Pleasure: A romantic comedy in three acts. London: Benn, 1925.

The King's Wooing: A play in one act. London and Glasgow: Gowans and Gray, 1929. Boston: Baker International Play Bureau, 1930.

Rope Enough: A play in three acts. Dublin and London: Maunsel, 1914.

Shakespeare's End; and other Irish plays. Prefatory letter to Joseph Conrad. London: Swift, 1912.

FICTION

Adam and Caroline: Being the sequel to 'Adam of Dublin.' London: Collins, 1921. New York: Harcourt, 1922.

Adam of Dublin: A romance of to-day. London: Collins; New York: Harcourt, 1920.

The Age of Miracles: A novel of our time. London: Collins, 1925.

In London: The story of Adam and marriage. London: Collins; New York: Harcourt, 1922.

Judith Quinn: A novel for women. Bristol: Arrowsmith, 1939.

Judith's Love. Bristol: Arrowsmith, 1940.

Married Life. London: Collins, 1924.

A Martial Medley: Fact and Fiction. Freeport, N.Y.: Books for Libraries, 1970.

Napoleon Passes. Intro. London: Arrowsmith, 1933.

The Pity of War. London: Glaisher, 1906.

Rowena Barnes. London: Collins, 1923.

Soldier Born: A story of youth. London: Collins, 1927.

Soldier of Waterloo: A story of manhood. London: Collins, 1928.

Soldier's End. [London]: Arrowsmith, 1938.

Soldier's Wife. [London]: Arrowsmith, 1935.

Yet Do Not Grieve. New York: Scribner, 1928.

Young Lady Dazingcourt: A discovery. London: Collins, 1926.

EDITED BY

With Charles Edmonds, W. W. Grundy, John Brophy, "Miles," Carrie Denison, Stephen Southwold, E. C. Pattison, Norman Hancock, Eric Partridge. *A Martial Melody: Fact and fiction.* London: Eric Partridge at the Scholartis Press, 1931. Freeport, N.Y.: Books For Libraries, 1970.

Patrick Henry Pearse (1879-1916)

For information about items marked Hyde see the note at the beginning of the list of Hyde's works.

COLLECTED AND SELECTED WORKS

*The Best of Pearse. Ed. by Proinsias MacAonghusa and Liam Ó Réagáin. Cork: Mercier, 1968.

Collected Works of Padraic H. Pearse. 3 vols. Vol. 1. *Plays, Stories, Poems.* Intro. by Patrick Browne. Dublin and London: Maunsel; New York: Stokes, 1917. Vol. 2. *Songs of the Irish Rebels and Specimens from an Irish Anthology.* Dublin and London: Maunsel; New York: Stokes, 1918. Vol. 3. *Political Writings and Speeches.*

Dublin and London: Maunsel and Roberts; New York: Stokes, 1922.

Collected Works by Padraic H. Pearse. 5 vols. Dublin, Cork, and Belfast: Phoenix, 1924. Vol. 1. *The Story of a Success and The Man Called Pearse.* Ed. Desmond Ryan. Vol. 2. *Scríbhinní.* Vol. 3. *Songs of the Irish Rebels and Specimens from an Irish Anthology: Some Aspects of Irish Literature.* Three Lectures on Gaelic Topics. Vol. 4. *Plays, Stories and Poems.* Vol. 5. *Political Writings and Speeches.* This ed. is identical to the one in the first entry.

Poems by P. H. Pearse. Dublin and London: Maunsel, 1918.

Scríbhinní. Collected Works in Gaelic. Dublin and London: Maunsel, 1919.

*Short Stories of Padraic Pearse. Ed. Desmond Maguire. Cork: Mercier, 1968. Irish and English.
The Singer; and other plays. Dublin and London: Maunsel, 1918.

INDIVIDUAL WORKS

*Amhrain Chuilm de Bhailis. Pref. by Seosamh Laoide and Douglas Hyde. 1903. Hyde 152.

An Mháthair agus sgéalta eile. Vocabulary by Peadar Ó Dubhda. Dundalk: Tempest, 1916. 2nd ed.

An Sgoil: A Direct Method Course in Irish. Part 1. Pref. Dublin and London: Maunsel [1913].

Bodach an Chóta Lachtna. Baile Átha Cliath: Connradh na Gaedhilge, 1906.

Bruidhean Chaorthainn: Sgéal Fionnaidheachta. Baile Átha Cliath: Connradh na Gaedhilge, 1908.

Copy of the Last Letter of P. H. Pearse to his Mother. n.p., n.d.

From a Hermitage. 2nd ed. Dublin: "Irish Freedom" Office, 1915.

Ghosts. Dublin: Whelan, 1916.

How Does She Stand? Three Addresses. Dublin: "Irish Freedom" Office, 1915. 2nd ed.

In First Century Ireland. Fore. Dublin and Cork: Talbot [1935]. London: Rich and Cowan, 1936.

Iosagan agus sgéalta eile. Baile Átha Cliath: Connradh na Gaedhilge, 1909. Same in English with the title *Iosagan; and other stories.* Trans. by Joseph Campbell. Dublin: Maunsel, 1918.

*Irish in a Dublin School. A report on the teaching of Irish in John Street National Schools. Dublin: By Miss K. Killeen and P. H. Pearse [1902]. Hyde 465.

The King: A morality. Dublin: Maunsel, 1922.

Last Letter and Poem of Padraic Pearse, First President of the Irish Republic. Written to his mother in Kilmainham Prison, Dublin, on May 3rd, 1916, shortly before his execution. [Dublin, 1916].

Maingín Scéal: Cnuasach de scéaltaib i gcomair an aosa óig ar n-a n-aitdhéanamh i nGaedhilge. Baile Átha Cliath agus Corcaigh: Clólucht an Tálboidigh [1936].

The Murder Machine. Dublin: Whelan, 1916.

Ós Cionn na Fairrge agus aistí eile. Baile Átha Cliath: Comhlucht Oideachais na hÉireann [1936].

Ó Pheann an Piarsaigh. i. Téasca toghaidhe as an Saothor literadha a rinn. Baile Átha Cliath agus Corcaigh: Comhlucht Oideachais na hÉireann [1946].

Poll an Phiobaire. Colm Ó Conaire. Pseud. Vocabulary. [Baile Átha Cliath]: Connradh na Gaedhilge, 1906.

The Separatist Idea. Dublin: Whelan, 1916.

Sgoil Éanna. St. Enda's School. An Clár, 1910-1911. Prospectus, *1910-1911.* Dublin: Dollard [1910]. Irish and English.

The Sovereign People. Dublin: Whelan, 1916.

The Spiritual Nation. Dublin: Whelan, 1916.

The Story of a Success. Being a record of St. Enda's College, September, 1908, to Easter 1916. Ed. Desmond Ryan. Dublin and London: Maunsel, 1920. O'Hegarty lists an ed. of 1917, but I have not seen a copy.

Suantraidhe agus Goltraidhe. Baile Átha Cliath: The Irish Review, 1914.

Three Lectures on Gaelic Topics. Pref. Dublin: Gill, 1898.

EDITED BY

An Macaomh. Ed. by Pearse and written by the Masters and Students of St. Enda's School. 1909-1913. Dublin: Kenny, 1909. Dublin: St. Enda's, 1910-1913.

Tadg ua Donnchada agus Pádraic Mac Piarais do chuir i n-eagar: An Taitriseoir. Baile Átha Cliath: Connradh na Gaedhilge, 1900-[1902].

BIBLIOGRAPHICAL, BIOGRAPHICAL, AND CRITICAL STUDIES

Coilin (pseud.). *Patrick H. Pearse: A sketch of his life.* Dublin: Curtis [1916].

Debroey, Steven. *Repel uit roeping: Het leven van ierse vrijiheitshedld Patrick Pearse.* Mit historische door Arthur de Bruyne. Tielt: Drukker-Uitgenrij, 1954.

Hayes, James. See Ó hAodha, Seamas.

Le Roux, Louis M. *L'Irlande Militante: La Vie de Patrice Pearse, avec une introduction historique et 15 photographies.* Rennes; Imprimerie de Bretagne, 1932. Same with the title *The Life of Pearse: Adapted from the French of Louis Le Roux and rev. by the author.* Trans. by Desmond Ryan. Dublin: Talbot, 1932.

McCay, Hedley. *Padraic Pearse: A new biography.* Cork: Mercier, 1966.

O'Farrell, William G. *An Appreciation of Padraic H. Pearse, First President of the Irish Republic.* New York: Connolly, 1919.

Ó hAodha, Seamus. *James Hayes. Pádraic Mac Piarias: Sgéaluidhe; Patrick H. Pearse: Storyteller.* Dublin: Talbot [1920]. Irish and English.

O'Hegarty, Patrick Sarsfield. *A Bibliography of the Books Written by P. H. Pearse.* Dublin: Pvt. Ptd. by Thom, 1931.

Ó Searcaigh, Seamus. *Pádraic Mac Piarias.* Baile Átha Cliath: Oifig an tSoláthair, 1938.

Porter, Raymond J. *P. H. Pearse.* New York: Twayne, 1973.

Regan, John X. (ed.). *What Made Sinn Fein: The chief political content of Pearse, the Gael of Gaels; something of MacNeill, Ireland's historian, Griffith, Ireland's statistician, and the O'Rahilly, a leader of the volunteers.* The result of a year's (1919) study in Ireland of Sinn Fein. Fore. Worcester, Massachusetts: Harrigan, 1921.

Ryan, Desmond. *The Man Called Pearse*. Dublin and London: Maunsel, 1919.

————. *Remembering Sion*. London: Miles, 1934.

Lennox Robinson (1886-1958)

COLLECTED AND SELECTED PLAYS

Killycreggs in Twilight; and other plays. London: Macmillan, 1939.

More Plays. New York: Macmillan, 1935.

Plays. London: Macmillan, 1928.

Two One-Act Comedies: Never the Time and the Place and Crabbed Youth and Age. Belfast: Carter, 1953.

Two Plays: Harvest; The Clancy Name. Dublin: Maunsel, 1911.

The White Blackbird and Portrait. Dublin and Cork: Talbot, 1926.

INDIVIDUAL PLAYS

The Big House: Four scenes in its life. London: Macmillan, 1928.

Church Street: A play. Belfast: Carter, 1955.

Crabbed Youth and Age: A little comedy. London and New York: Putnam, 1924.

The Cross-Roads: A play in a prologue and two acts. Dublin: Maunsel, 1909.

Drama at Inish: An exaggeration in three acts. See *Is Life Worth Living?*

The Dreamers: A play in three acts. London and Dublin: Maunsel, 1915.

Ever the Twain: A comedy in three acts. London: Macmillan, 1930.

The Far-Off Hills: A comedy in three acts. London: Chatto and Windus, 1931. New York: Macmillan, 1932.

Give a Dog—: A play in three acts. London: Macmillan, 1928.

Is Life Worth Living? An exaggeration in three acts. London: Macmillan, 1933. Rev. ed., New York, Los Angeles, London, and Toronto: French, 1938. Same with title *Drama at Inish. An exaggeration in three acts.* Dublin: Duffy, 1953.

The Lost Leader: A play in three acts. Dublin: Thomas Kiersey at the Eigeas Press, 1918.

The Lucky Finger: A comedy in three acts. New York, Hollywood, London, and Toronto: French, 1949.

Patriots: A play in three acts. Dublin and London: Maunsel; Boston: Luce, 1912.

Pictures in a Theatre: A conversation piece. Dublin: Abbey Theatre [1947].

The Round Table: A comedy tragedy in three acts. London and New York: Putnam, 1924.

The White Blackbird. Dublin and Cork: Talbot [1926].

The Whiteheaded Boy: A comedy in three acts. Intro. by Ernest Boyd. New York: French; London and New York: Putnam, 1921. Dublin: Talbot [1922].

NON-FICTION

Bryan Cooper. London: Constable, 1931.

Curtain Up: An autobiography. London: Joseph, 1942.

Dark Days: Sketches of life in Ireland. Dublin: Talbot; London: Unwin, 1918.

Ireland's Abbey Theatre: A History, 1899-1951. London: Sidgwick and Jackson, 1951. Port Washington, New York: Kennikat, 1968.

Ireland's Abbey Theatre. New York and Los Angeles: French, n.d. (19 pp. only.)

I Sometimes Think. Dublin: Talbot, 1956.

Palette and Plough. Dublin: Browne and Nolan for the Richview Press, 1948.

Towards an Appreciation of the Theatre. Dublin: Metropolitan, 1945.

FICTION

Eight Short Stories. Dublin: Talbot; London: Unwin [1920].

A Young Man from the South. Dublin and London: Maunsel, 1917.

JOINT AUTHOR

With Tom Robinson and Nora Dorman. *Three Homes. These memories of childhood and youth are recalled by three members of an unimportant Irish family*. Fore. by Lennox Robinson. London: Joseph, 1938.

EDITED BY

Further Letters of John Butler Yeats. Sel. and with an intro. Dublin: Cuala, 1920. 400 copies.

A Golden Treasury of Irish Verse. London and New York: Macmillan, 1925.

Gregory, Isabella Augusta. *Lady Gregory's Journals*, 1916-1930. Intro. London: Putnam, 1946. New York: Macmillan, 1947.

The Irish Theatre: Lectures delivered during the Abbey Theatre Festival held in Dublin in August, 1938. Fore. London: Macmillan, 1939.

A Little Anthology of Modern Irish Verse. Sel. with a pref. Dublin: Cuala, 1928. 300 copies.

With Donagh MacDonagh. *Oxford Book of Irish Verse: XVII Century—XXth Century*. Pref. by Lennox Robinson. Intro. by Donagh Mac-Donagh. Oxford: Clarendon, 1958.

Parnell, Thomas. *Poems by Thomas Parnell*. Sel. and with a fore. Dublin: Cuala, 1927.

CRITICAL AND BIOGRAPHICAL STUDIES

O'Neill, M. J. *Lennox Robinson*. New York: Twayne, 1964.

W. R. Rodgers (1909-1969)

POETRY

Awake! and other poems. London: Secker and Warburg; New York: Harcourt, 1941.

Europa and the Bull; and other poems. London: Secker and Warburg, 1952.

PROSE

Ireland in Colour: A collection of forty colour photographs. Intro., text, and notes on the illustrations. London: Batsford; New York: Studio Publications in assoc. with Thomas Y. Crowell, 1957.

The Ulstermen and Their Country. London: Pub. for the British Council by Longmans, Green [1947].

BIOGRAPHY AND CRITICISM

O'Brien, Darcy. *W. R. Rogers.* (Irish Writers Series). Lewisburg, Pa.: Bucknell University [n.d].

George William Russcll, pseud.: AE (1867-1935)

STANDARD BIBLIOGRAPHY

Denson, Alan. *Printed Writings by George W. Russell (AE): A bibliography with some notes on his pictures and portraits.* Fore. by Padraic Colum. *Reminiscences of AE by M. J. Bonn. A note on AE and painting by Thomas Bockin.* Evanston, Ill., and London: Northwestern University, 1961.

PROSE

Selected Essays on Literary Subjects. Havertown, Pa.: Richard West, 1973.

BIBLIOGRAPHICAL, BIOGRAPHICAL, AND CRITICAL STUDIES

*Beins, Friedrich. *"AE" George William Russell: Sein Leben und Werk im Lichte seiner Theosophischen Weltanschauung.* Greifswald: n.p., 1934.

Clyde, William M. *A.E.* Fore. by Seamas O'Sullivan. Edinburgh and London: Moray, 1935.

Coates, C. C. *Some Less-Known Chapters in the Life of A.E. (George Russell): Being the substance of a lecture delivered at Belfast, November, 1936.* Dublin: Pvt. ptd. by Thom, 1939.

Eglinton, John (pseud. of W. K. Megee). *A Memoir of A.E. George William Russell.* Pref. London: Macmillan, 1937.

Figgis, Darrell. *A.E. (George W. Russell): A study of a man and a nation.* Dublin and London: Maunsel, 1916.

Hoepf'l, Heinz. *A.E.—George William Russell: Dichtung und Mystik.* Bonn: Bonner Studien zur englischen Philologie, P. Hanstein, 1935.

Johnson, Raynor C. *The Light and the Gate.* (On George W. Russell, Ambrose Pratt, the Venerable Sumangalo and Leslie D. Weatherhead. With Portraits.) London: Hodder and Stoughton, 1964.

Merchant, Francis. *A.E.: An Irish Promethean.* A study of the contribution of George William Russell to world culture. Columbia, S. C.: Benedict College, 1954.

O'Brien, James and Kain, Richard M. *George Russell AE.* (Irish Writers Series). Lewisburg, Pa.: Bucknell University (in prep.).

Plass, Martin. *Mystiche Lyrik und Politische Prosa im Werk George William Russell's—A.E.* Wurzburg: n.p., 1940.

Williams, David J. *A.E. George William Russell a Chymru.* Gwasg Aberystwyth: Llandysul, 1929.

George Bernard Shaw (1856-1950)

Since the bibliography of Shaw is so extensive and its history is so complex, this list is only a bibliography of major first editions. For thorough treatment of the Shavian bibliography see Dan Laurence's *A Bibliography of the Writings of George Bernard Shaw.*

BIBLIOGRAPHY

"Continuing Checklist of Shaviana," *The Shaw Review.* According to E. E. Stokes, Jr., the checklist "First appeared in Volume I, Number 2 (Autumn, 1951) of the old *Shaw Bulletin.* It was continued, in expanded form, when the *Bulletin* became *The Shaw*

Review (Volume II, Number 7, January, 1959) and has appeared, in some form compiled by successive bibliographers, in every successive issue to date."

Laurence, Dan H. *A Bibliography of the Writings of George Bernard Shaw*. London: Hart-Davis, in prep.

COLLECTED EDITIONS

Bernard Shaw and Karl Marx: A Symposium, 1884-1889. New York: Georgion, 1930. Limited Edition.

Bernard Shaw's Non-Dramatic Literary Criticism. Ed. S. Weintraub. Lincoln: Univ. of Nebr., 1972.

The Bodley Head Bernard Shaw: Collected plays w/ their prefaces. London: Bodley Head; London: M. Reinhardt, 1970.

Collected Works of G. B. Shaw. 33 Vols. Ed. Ayot St. Lawrence (1-30). New York: Wm. F. Wise, 1930-32.

How to Become a Musical Critic. Ed. by Dan H. Laurence. London: Hart-Davis, 1960. New York: Hill and Wang, 1961.

The Matter with Ireland. Ed. by Dan H. Laurence and David H. Greene. London: Hart-Davis. New York: Hill & Wang, 1962.

Plays of Bernard Shaw. 12 Vols. London: n.p., 1927.

The Religious Speeches of Bernard Shaw. Ed. by W. S. Smith. University Park: Pa. State U., 1963.

Road to Equality: 10 cup lectures and Essays 1884-1919. Ed. L. Crompton. Boston: Beacon, 1971.

Selected Non-Dramatic Writings. Ed. Dan H. Laurence. Boston: Houghton Mifflin, 1965.

Selected Novels of G. Bernard Shaw. Intro. by Arthur Ziegler. (n.p.): Caxton House, 1946. (Contains first book publication of serial text of *The Irrational Knot*.)

Shaw and Society: An Anthology and a Symposium. Ed. C. E. M. Joad. London: Odhams, 1953.

Shaw on Religion. Ed. W. S. Smith. London: Constable; New York: Dodd, Mead, 1967.

Shaw on Shakespeare: An Anthology of Bernard Shaw's Writings on the Plays and Productions of Shakespeare. New York: Dutton, 1961; London: Cassell, 1962.

Shaw's Complete Plays and Prefaces. 6 Vols. New York: Dodd, Mead, 1962. (Textually inaccurate.)

Short Stories, Scraps and Shavings. London: Constable, 1934.

Standard Edition of the Works of Bernard Shaw. 35 Vols. London: Constable, 1931-51.

Ten Short Plays. New York: Dodd, Mead, 1960.
Works of Bernard Shaw. Limited Edition. London: Constable, 1930. (1025 copies).

DRAMATIC FICTION

Plays are listed individually and are cross-referenced to the volume in which they occurred.

The Admirable Bashville, or Constancy Unrewarded. (w/ rev. ed. *Cashel Byron's Profession*). London: Grant Richards; Chicago: H. S. Stone, 1901. Also in *Translations and Tom Fooleries.*

Androcles and the Lion. London: Constable; New York: Brentano's, 1916. (pbd. w/ *Pygmalion* and *Overruled*). Alphabet ed. London: Penguin; Baltimore: Penguin, 1962.

The Apple Cart: A Political Extravaganza. London: Constable, New York: Brentano's, 1930.

Arms and the Man. (in Vol. II of *Plays, Pleasant and Unpleasant.*)

Back to Methuselah: A Metabiological Pentateuch. London: Constable, New York: Brentano's, 1921. (revised w/ ps.) London: Oxford University, 1945.

Brassbound's Conversion. (in *Three Plays for Puritans*).

Bouyant Billions. London: Constable; New York: Dodd, Mead, 1951. (Pbd. w/ *Farfetched Fables & Shakes versus Shaw.*)

Buoyant Billions. London: Constable, 1949 (1950). (Ltd. ed.)

Caesar and Cleopatra. (in *Three Plays for Puritans.*)

Candida. (in Vol. II of *Plays, Pleasant and Unpleasant.*)

Cymbelina Refinished. (Pbd. w/ *Geneva* and *Good King Charles.*) See *Geneva.*

The Dark Lady of the Sonnets. (Pbd. w/ *Misalliance* and *Fanny's First Play.*) See *Misalliance.*

The Devil's Disciple. (in *Three Plays for Puritans.*)

The Doctor's Dilemma. London: Constable; New York: Brentano's, 1911. (Pbd. w/ *Getting Married* and *The Shewing-Up of Blanco Posnet.*)

Fanny's First Play. (Pbd. w/ *Misalliance* and *The Dark Lady of the Sonnets*); see *Misalliance.*

Farfetched Fables. (Pbd. w/ *Buoyant Billions* and *Shakes versus Shaw*); see *Buoyant Billions.*

The Fascinating Foundling. (in *Translations and Tom Fooleries.*)

Gadfly. Bernard Shaw's Collected Plays. Vol. 7. London: Bodley Head, 1974. (Fragment of the *Cassone, Fugitive Playlets and Dialogues, Passion Play.*)

Geneva. London: Constable, 1946 [1947]. New York: Dodd, Mead, 1947. (Pbd. w/ *Cymbeline Refinished* and *Good King Charles.*)

Getting Married. (Pbd. w/ *The Doctor's Dilemma* and *The Shewing-Up of Blanco Posnet*); see *The Doctor's Dilemma.*

The Glimpse of Reality. (in *Translations and Tom Fooleries.*)

Good King Charles. (Pbd. w/ *Cymbeline Refinished* and *Geneva*); see *Geneva.*

Great Catherine. (Pbd. w/ *Heartbreak House* and *Playlets of the War*); see *Heartbreak House.*

Heartbreak House. London: Constable; New York: Brentano's, 1919. (Pbd. w/ *Great Catherine* and *Playlets of the War*).

How He Lied to Her Husband. (Pbd. w/ *Major Barbara* and *John Bull's Other Island*); see *John Bull's Other Island.*

Jitta's Atonement. (in *Translations and Tom Fooleries.*)

John Bull's Other Island. London: Constable; New York: Brentano's, 1907. (Pbd. w/ *Major Barbara* and *How He Lied to Her Husband.*)

Major Barbara. (Pbd. w/ *John Bull's Other Island* and *How He Lied to Her Husband*); see *John Bull's Other Island.*

Man and Superman: A Comedy and a Philosophy. Westminster: Constable, 1903. New York: Brentano's, 1904. (w/ textual varieties.) Revised. London: Constable, 1931.

The Man of Destiny. (in Vol. II of *Plays, Pleasant and Unpleasant.*)

The Millionairess. (in *Three New Plays.*)

Misalliance. London: Constable; New York: Brentano's, 1914. (Pbd. w/ *The Dark Lady of the Sonnets* and *Fanny's First Play.*)

Mrs. Warren's Profession: A Play in Four Acts. London: G. Richards, 1902. (Stage Soc. Ed. w/ author's apology; First pbd. in *Plays Unpleasant*, 1898; the Apology alone w/ introduction by J. Corbun, *The Tyranny of Police and Press*, New York, 1905). New York: Brentano's, 1903.

Mrs. Warren's Profession. (in Vol. I of *Plays, Pleasant and Unpleasant.*)

The Musical Cure. (in *Translations and Tom Fooleries.*)

Overruled: a Dramatic Study. London: Constable; New York: Brentano's, 1916; London: Constable, 1913. (Pbd. w/ *Pygmalion* and *Androcles and the Lion.*)

On the Rocks. (Pbd. w/ *Too True to be Good* and *Village Wooing.*)

Passion Play: A Dramatic Fragment, 1878. Ed. G. E. Bringle (Ltd. Ed.). Iowa City: Windhover Press. London: Bertram Rota, 1971.

Passion, Poison, and Petrifaction, or the Fatal Gazogene. (First pbd. in H. Furniss's *Christmas Annual*, ——, 1905); (also in *Translations and Tom Fooleries*).

The Philanderer. (in Vol. I of *Plays, Pleasant and Unpleasant.*)

Playlets of the War. (Pbd. w/ *Heartbreak House* and *Great Catherine*); see *Heartbreak House.*

Plays, Pleasant and Unpleasant. (2 volumes.) London: Grant Richards. Chicago: H. S. Stone, 1898. (Vol. I: *P. Unpleasant: Widower's House, Mrs. Warren's Profession, The Philanderer*; Vol. II: *P. Pleasant: Arms and the Man, Candida, The Man of Destiny, You Never Can Tell.*)

Press Cuttings. (in *Translations and Tom Fooleries.*)

Pygmalion. London: Constable; New York: Brentano's, 1916; (Pbd. w/ *Androcles and the Lion* and *Overruled.*)

Saint Joan. A Chronicle Play in Six Scenes and an Epilogue. London: Constable; New York: Brentano's, 1924.

Shakes versus Shaw. (Pbd. w/ *Farfetched Fables* and *Buoyant Billions*); see *Buoyant Billions.*

The Shewing-Up of Blanco Posnet. (Pbd. w/ *The Doctor's Dilemma* and *Getting Married*); see *The Doctor's Dilemma.*

The Simpleton of the Unexpected Isles. (in *Three New Plays.*)

Sixteen Self-sketches. New York: Dodd, Mead; London: Constable, 1949.

The Six of Calais. (in *Three New Plays.*)

Three New Plays: The Simpleton of the Unexpected Isles, The Six of Calais, The Millionairess. London: Constable; New York: Dodd, Mead, 1936.

Three Plays For Puritans: The Devil's Disciple, Caesar and Cleopatra, and *Captain Brassbound's Conversion.* London: Grant Richards, New York: H. S. Stone, 1901.

Translations and Tom Fooleries. London: Constable; New York: Brentano's, 1926. (Contents: *Jitta's Atonement*; *The Admirable Bashville*; *Press Cuttings*; *The Glimpse of Reality*; *Passion, Poison, and Petrification; The Fascinating Foundling; The Music Cure.*)

Too True to be Good. London: Constable; New York: Dodd, Mead, 1934. (Pbd. w/ *Village Wooing* and *On the Rocks.*)

Village Wooing. (Pbd. w/ *Too True to Be Good* and *On the Rocks*); see *Too True to Be Good.*

Why She Should Not. (in *Ten Short Plays.*)

Widower's House: A Comedy. London: Henry & Co., 1893.

Widower's House. Rev. in Vol. I of *Plays, Pleasant and Unpleasant.*

You Never Can Tell. (in Vol. II of *Plays, Pleasant and Unpleasant.*)

NON-FICTION

There has been no attempt to list all of the separate Fabian tracts.

The Alleged Collapse of Socialism. (in *Everyman; his life, work, and books.*) London: Everyman, 1912.

Anarchism Versus State Socialism. London: "Alabm" Publishing Co., 1896.

Bernard Shaw and Facism. London: Favil, 1927.

Bernard Shaw's ready reconer: a guide to civilization. Ed. by N. H. Leigh-Taylor. New York: Random House, 1965. London: Peter Owen, 1966.

The Crime of Imprisonment. New York: Philosophical Library, 1946.

The Common Sense of Municipal Trading. Westminster: Constable, 1904; London: Fifield, 1908. (w/ new preface.)

The Crisis and the Social Function of Art and Science. London: George Allen and Unwin, 1943.

Doctors' Delusions, Crude Criminology, and Sham Education. London: Constable, 1932. (St. Edition). London: Constable, 1931. (Limited Edition).

Do We Agree: A debate between G. K. Chesterton and Bernard Shaw with Hilaire Belloc in the Chair. London: Palmer; Hartford: Michael, 1928.

Essays in Fabian Socialism. London: Constable, 1930. Standard Edition.

Everybody's Political What's What? London: Constable; New York: Dodd, Mead, 1944.

Fabian Essays in Socialism. London: London Fabian Soc. 1889. New York: Humboldt, 1891 (unauthorized), Jubilee Edition. London: Allen & Unwin, 1948.

Fabianism and the Empire: A Manifesto. London: Grant Richards, 1900.

The Future of Political Science in America: A Lecture. New York: Dodd, Mead, 1933.

How to Settle the Irish Question. Dublin: Talbot; London: Constable, 1917.

Immaturity. London: Constable, 1931. (Vol I. Standard.)

"Imprisonment." Preface to *English Prisons under Local Government*. by Beatrice and Sidney Webb. Pvt. Pt. London: Constable, 1922. New York: Brentano's, 1925.

In Good King Charles' Golden Days: A history lesson. London: Constable, 1939.

The Intelligent Woman's Guide to Socialism and Capitalism. London: Constable, 1928; New York: Brentano's; Garden City, New York: Garden City Publishing Co., 1928. (London: 1929 w/ new introduction.)

Last Will and Testament. Foreword by Wm. D. Chase. Flint, Mich.: Appletree Press, 1954. (also reprinted in A. Chapelow's *"The Chucker-Out."*)

"A Little Talk on America." London: Friends of the Soviet Union; Okla. City: American Guardian, 1931. (unauthorized)

"The Nun and the Dramatist: Dame Laurentia McLachlan and George Bernard Shaw" *Cornhill Magazine,* CLXVIII (1956), 415-58. Also, *Tribute to Dame Laurentia McLachlan by the Benedictines of Staudbrook.* London: Hutchinson's, 1956.

"On Going to Church." E. Aurora, New York: Roycraft shop, 1896. (unauthorized). Boston: Luce, 1905 (var. text). First pub. *Savoy,* January, 1896; Riverside, Conn.: R. C. Busch, 1915. (unauthorized.)

On Language. London: Citadel, 1925.

On Modern Composition. London: Craven, 1921.

Our Theatres in the Nineties. 3 volumes. Standard Edition. London: Constable, 1932, 1931, ltd. ed.

Peace Conference Hints. London: Constable, 1919.

Press Cuttings, A Topical Sketch compiled from the Editorial and Correspondence Columns of the Daily Papers. London: Constable, 1909; New York: Brentano's, 1913. (Note: 50 Copyright copies printed in 1909.) See *Translations and Tom Fooleries.*

The Political Madhouse in America and Nearer Home. London: Constable, 1933.

The Rationalization of Russia by George Bernard Shaw. Ed. by H. M. Geduld. Bloomington: Indiana University, 1964.

Ruskin's Politics. London: Ruskin Centenary Council, 1921. 1st in U. S. in *Platform and Pulpit.*

Rhyming Picture Guide to Ayot St. Lawrence. Luton: Ledgrave, 1950.

Shaw: Autobiography. Vol. I: 1856-1899. New York: Weybright and Talley, 1969. London: Max Rheinhardt, 1920. Vol. II: 1898-1950; New York: Weybright and Talley, 1970; London: Max Rheinhardt, 1971.

Shaw Gives Himself Away: an Autobiographical Miscellany. Newton: Greynog Press, 1939.

Shaw on Censorship. London: Shaw Society, 1955. (Shavian Tract #3).

Ab. Taubert. *Shaw on Language.* New York: Philosophical Lib., 1963. London: Peter Owen, 1965.

Shaw on Vivisection. Ed. by G. H. Bowker. London: Allen and Unwin, 1949; Chicago: Althea, 1951.

Shaw. "The Chucker-Out": a biographical exposition and critique. Ed. by Allen Chapellow. London: Allen and Unwin, 1969. New York: Amass, 1971.

Socialism of Shaw. ed. by James Fuchs. New York: Vanguard, 1927.

Socialism and Superior Brains. London: Fabian Society, 1909. London: A. C. Fifield; New York: Lane, 1910.

Table-Talk of G. B. S. by Archibald Henderson. New York: Harper; London: Chapman and Hall, 1925.

William Morris: artist, writer, and Socialist. Oxford: Blackwell, 1936.

William Morris as I Knew Him. New York: Dodd, Mead, 1936.

What I Really Wrote About the War. London: Constable, 1931. (standard edition); (1930, lit. ed.) New York: Wise, 1932. See also: *Common Sense about the War.*

LETTERS

There has been no attempt to include all letters—only those published in book or pamphlet form.

Advice to a Young Critic and Other Letters. Notes and Introduction by E. J. West. New York: Crain, 1955. London: Peter Owen, 1956 (w/o West's Notes); London: 1933.

Bernard Shaw and Mrs. Patrick Campbell: Their Correspondence. London: V. Gollancz; New York: Knopf, 1952.

Bernard Shaw's Letters to Granville Barker. Ed. C. B. Purdom. London: Phoenix House; New York: Theatre Arts Books, 1957.

Collected Letters. Ed. by Dan H. Laurence. Vol. I (1874-1897). London: Max Reinhardt; New York: Dodd, Mead, 1965. Vol. II (1898-1910). London: Max Reinhardt; New York: Dodd, Mead, 1972.

Ellen Terry and Bernard Shaw: A Correspondence. Ed. by Christopher St. John. Preface by Shaw. New York: Theatre Arts Books, 1949.

Ellen Terry and Bernard Shaw: A Correspondence. With preface by Shaw. Ltd. Ed. London: Constable; New York: Fountain Press,

1931. Trade Edition. (3000 numbered copies). London: Constable, 1931; New York: Putnam, 1931.

Florence Farr, Bernard Shaw, and W. B. Yeats (letters). Ed. by Clifford Bax. Dublin: Cools Press, Ltd. Ed., 1941. New York: Dodd, Mead, 1942. London: Home and Van Tal, 1946.

A Letter from Bernard Shaw to J. C. Williamson. Cremore, N. S. Wales: Talkarra, 1955. (with preface note by W. W. Stone.) Ltd. Ed.

Letters from George Bernard Shaw to Miss Alma Murray. Edinburgh: Dunneden, 1927. (30 copies.) *More Letters*; Edinburgh: Dunneden, 1932.

My Dear Dorothea: A Practical System of Moral Education for Females Embodied in a Letter to a Young Person of that Sex. London: Phoenix House, 1956. New York: Vanguard, 1957.

To a Young Actress: The Letters of Bernard Shaw to Molly Tompkins. London: Constable; New York: Clarkson Potter, 1960.

NON-DRAMATIC FICTION

Adventures of the Black Girl in her Search for God. London: Constable; New York: Dodd, Mead, 1932.

Black Girl in Search of God. in Standard Edition of Shaw's *Short Stories, Scraps and Shavings*. London: Constable, 1932.

Cashel Byron's Profession. London: Modern, 1886; New York: H. S. Stone, 1901 (rev.). For dramatic version see *The Admirable Bashville*. London: Walter Scott, 1889 (rev.) Note: 3 unauthorized American versions. New York: George Munro, 1886. New York: Harper, 1886. New York: Brentano's, 1899.

The Irrational Knot. London: Constable; New York: Brentano's, 1905. First pbd. in *Our Corner*, 1885-7 from manuscript. See *Selected Novels*. (n.p.): Caxton, 1946.

Love among the Artists. London: Constable, 1914; Chicago: H. S. Stone, 1900. First Pbd. in *Our Corner*, 1887-8.

An Unfinished Novel. Ed. by Stanley Weintraub. New York: Dodd, Mead, 1950. Ltd. Ed. London: Constable, 1958.

An Unsocial Socialist. London: Swan Sonnenschein, 1887; New York: Brentano's 1888. w/ added appendix. (N. Y.: Brentano's, 1908. unauthorized). First pbd. in *Today*, 1884.

CRITICISM

These are critical studies by Shaw. For criticism about Shaw, see the "Continuing Checklist of Shaviana" in the *Shaw Review*.

The Art of Rehearsal. New York: S. French, 1928.

The Author's Apology From Mrs. Warren's Profession. New York: Brentano's, 1905.

Dramatic Opinions and Essays; with an Apology. New York: Brentano's, 1906 (unauthorized). New York: Brentano's, 1907 (w/ new preface). 2 Vols. London: Constable, 1907.

Interlude at the Playhouse. In *Daily Mail*, 29 Nov. 1905. Also, in C. Maude's *Behind the Scenes w/ Cecil Maude*. London: John Murray, 1927. C. Maude's *Lest I Forget*. New York: J. A. Sears, 1928.

London Music in 1888-89. London: Constable; New York: Dodd, Mead, 1937.

London Music, 1890-1894. London: Constable, 1932. Limited Edition, 1931.

Pen Portraits and Reviews. Collected Ed.: New York: Wise & Co., 1931; Standard Ed.: London: Constable, 1932. Limited Edition: London: Constable, 1931.

The Perfect Wagnerite. London: Grant Richards, 1898; Chicago: H. S. Stone, 1899; revised w/ new preface, London: Grant Richards, 1902; New York: Brentano's, 1909; London: Constable, 1913; London: Constable, 1923. Vol. 19. See *Major Critical Essays* in St. Ed. and Col. Ed.

Preface to 3 plays by Brieux. New York: Brentano's, 1910.

The Quintessence of Ibsenism. London: Walter Scott, 1891, 1913; Boston: B. Tucker, 1891 (unauth.); New York: Brentano's, 1904 (unauth.); London: Constable, 1913 (rev.); New York: Brentano's, 1913 (rev.); London: Constable, 1922, w/ new preface. Vol. 19 St. Edition in *Major Critical Essays*, 1931.

The Sanity of Art. London: Constable, 1908 (rev.); New York: B. Tucker, 1908. In *Major Critical Essays*-Vol. 19. in St. Ed. and Coll. Ed.

Shaw on Theatre. Ed. E. J. West. New York: Hill and Wang, 1958. [Devby Luu, 1959]; London: MacGibbon and Kee, 1959.

Edith OEnone Somerville (1858-1949) and Martin Ross, pseud. of Violet Florence Martin (1862-1915)

STANDARD BIBLIOGRAPHY

Cummins, Geraldine Dorothy. *Dr. E. OE. Somerville: A biography.* Being the first biography of the leading member of the famous literary partnership of E. OE. Somerville and Martin Ross, with a new bibliography of first editions compiled by Robert Vaughan and a preface by Lennox Robinson. London: Drakers, 1952.

BIBLIOGRAPHICAL, BIOGRAPHICAL AND CRITICAL STUDIES ABOUT

Collis, Maurice. *Somerville and Ross.* London: Faber and Faber, 1968.

Cronin, John. *Somerville and Ross.* (Irish Writers Series). Lewisburg, Pa.: Bucknell University, 1972.

Fehlmann, Guy. *Somerville et Ross, témoins de l'Irlande d'hier.* Caen: Association des Publications de la Faculté des Lettres de Sciences Humaines de l'Université de Caen, 1970.

Hudson, Elizabeth. *A Bibliography of the First Editions of the Works of E. OE. Somerville and Martin Ross.* Explanatory notes by E. OE. Somerville. New York: The Sport Gallery and Bookshop, 1942. 300 numbered and signed copies.

Powell, Lady Violet Georgiana. *The Irish Cousins: The books and background of Somerville and Ross.* London: Heinemann, 1970.

Somerville and Ross: A Symposium. Belfast: Queen's University, Institute of Irish Studies, 1969.

James Stephens (1882-1950)

STANDARD BIBLIOGRAPHY

Bransbäck, Birgit (Johannson). *James Stephens: A literary and biographical study.* Upsala: Lundequist; Cambridge: Harvard University, 1959.

RECENT PUBLICATIONS OF STEPHENS'S WRITINGS

James, Seumas and Jacques: Unpublished Writings of James Stephens. Chosen and ed. with an intro. by Lloyd Frankenberg. With a list of broadcasts by James Stephens. London and New York: Macmillan, 1964.

James Stephens: A Selection. Sel. with an intro. by Lloyd Frankenberg. Pref. by Padraic Colum. London: Macmillan, 1962. Pub. in the U.S.A. with title *A James Stephens Reader.* New York: Macmillan, 1962.

*A Singing Wind. Selected Poems. Ed. Quail Hawkins. Drawings by Harold Goodwin. New York: Macmillan, 1968.

BIBLIOGRAPHICAL, BIOGRAPHICAL, AND CRITICAL STUDIES ABOUT

Bransbäck, Birgit. *James Stephens.* (Irish Writers Series). Lewisburg, Pa.: Bucknell University [n.d.]

Cary, Richard, editor. "A Tribute to James Stephens, Waterville, Maine 1961," *Colby Library Quarterly*, V, 9 (March 1961).

Martin, Augustine. *James Stephens.* Chester Springs: Dufour (in prep.).

Poepping, Hilde. *James Stephens. Eine Untersuchung über die irische Erneuerungs bewegung in der Zeil von 1900-1930.* Halle: Deutsche Gesselschaft für keltische Studien, 1940.

Pyle, Hilary. *James Stephens: His work and an account of his life.* London: Routledge and Kegan Paul, 1965.

Rattray, R. *Poets in the Flesh: Tagore, Yeats, Dunsany, Stephens, [and] Drinkwater.* Cambridge: Golden Head, 1961.

Royal Society of Literature of the United Kingdom, London Academic Committee. *Award of the Edmond de Polignac Prize to James Stephens by W. B. Yeats.* Friday, November 28, 1913. London: n.p., 1914.

Saul, G. B. *Withdrawn in Gold: Three Commentaries on Genius.* The Hague: Mouton, 1970.

Williams, Lolo Aneurin. *John Collings Squire and James Stephens.* (Bibliographies of their works.) With a prefatory letter by J. C. Squire. London: Chaundy, 1922.

Francis Stuart (1902-   )

FICTION

Angel of Pity. London: Grayson, 1935.

Angels of Providence. London: Gollancz; Toronto: Doubleday, 1959.

Black List/ Section H. With preface and postscript by Harry T. Moore. Carbondale: Southern Illinois University, 1971.

Bridge. London: Collins, 1937.

Chariot. London: Gollancz, 1953.

Coloured Dome. London: Gollancz, 1932. New York: Macmillan, 1933.

Flowering Cross. London: Gollancz, 1950.

Glory. London: Gollancz, 1933.

Good Friday's Daughter. London: Gollancz, 1952.

Great Squire. London: Collins, 1939.

Immortal Wings. London: Crowther, 1943.

In Search of Love. London: Collins; New York: Macmillan, 1935.

Julie. New York: Knopf, 1938. London: Collins, 1939.

Pigeon Irish. London: Gollancz; New York: Macmillan, 1932.

Pilgrimage. London: Gollancz, 1955.

Pillar of Cloud. London: Gollancz, 1948.

Redemption. London: Gollancz, 1949. New York: Devin-Adair, 1950.

Try the Sky. Fore. by Compton Mackenzie. London: Gollancz; New York: Macmillan, 1933.

Victors and Vanquished. London: Gollancz, 1958. Cleveland: Pennington; Toronto: Doubleday, 1959.

White Hare. London: Collins; New York: Macmillan, 1936.

Women and God: A novel. London: Cape, 1931.

NON-FICTION

Lecture on Nationality and Culture. Baile Átha Cliath: Sinn Féin árd-Chomhairle, 1924.

Mystics and Mysticism. Dublin: Catholic Truth Society of Ireland, 1929.

Racing for Pleasure and Profit in Ireland and Elsewhere. Dublin and Cork: Talbot [1937].

Things to Live For: Notes for an autobiography. London: Cape, 1934. New York: Macmillan, 1935.

POEMS (Written and published under the name of H. Stuart)

We Have Kept Faith. Dublin: Pvt. ptd., 1923.

BIOGRAPHY AND CRITICISM

McCormick, William J., Editor. *Francis Stuart: A Festschrift for His Seventieth Birthday.* Dublin: Dolmen, 1972.

Natterstad, J. H. *Francis Stuart.* (Irish Writers Series). Lewisburg, Pa.: Bucknell University, 1974.

John Millington Synge (1871-1909)

BIBLIOGRAPHY

Collected Works. Vol. 5. London: Oxford University Press (in prep.).

Levitt, Paul. *John Millington Synge: A Bibliography of Criticism.* New York: Barnes and Noble, 1973.

COLLECTED WORKS

Collected Works. Vol. 5. London: Oxford University Press (in prep.). Vol. 1, *Prose*, and Vol. 2, *Poetry*, 1962. Vols. 3 and 4, *Plays*, 1968. Vol. 5, Bibliography, (in prep.).

RECENT PROSE

An Autobiography of J. M. Synge: Constructed from the manuscripts by Alan Price. Dublin: Dolmen, 1965. 1250 copies.

Emerald Apex. A selection of J. M. Synge's studies of Irish people and places with intro., notes and exercises by Alan Price. London and Glasgow: Blackie, 1966.

LETTERS

Letters to Molly: John Millington Synge to Maire O'Neill, 1906-1909. Ed. by Ann Saddlemyer. Cambridge, Mass.: Harvard University, 1971.

Some letters of John M. Synge to Lady Gregory and W. B. Yeats. Selected by Ann Saddlemyer. Dublin: Cuala, 1971. 500 copies.

*Some unpublished letters and documents of J. M. Synge formerly in the possession of Mr. Lawrence Wilson of Montreal and now for the first time published for him by the Redpath Press, Montreal, 1959. "Limited to 250 copies."

PHOTOGRAPHS

My Wallet of Photographs: The Collected Photographs of J. M. Synge. Arranged and introduced by Lile Stephens. Dublin: Dolmen, 1971.

TRANSLATED BY

J. M. Synge—Translations. Ed. from original manuscripts by Robin Skelton. Dublin: Dolmen, 1961. Reprinted with additions from the original works.

BIBLIOGRAPHICAL, BIOGRAPHICAL, AND CRITICAL STUDIES

*Aufhauser, Annemarie. *Sind die Dramen von John Millington Synge durch französische Vorbilder beeinflusst.* Würzburg: n.p., 1935.

Bickley, Francis Lawrence. *J. M. Synge and The Irish Dramatic Movement.* London, Boston, and New York: Houghton Mifflin, 1912.

Bougeois, Maurice. *John Millington Synge and the Irish Theatre.* London: Constable, 1913.

Bushrui, Suheil B., editor. *Sunshine and the Moon's Delight: A Centenary Tribute to John Millington Synge, 1871-1909.* London: Smythe; New York: Barnes & Noble, 1972.

Corkery, Daniel. *Synge and Anglo Irish Literature: A study.* Dublin and Cork: Cork University Press with the Educational Company of Ireland; New York: Longmans, Green, 1931.

Coxhead, Eilen Elizabeth. *J. M. Synge and Lady Gregory*. London and New York: Longmans, Green, 1962.

Estill, A. D. *The Sources of Synge*. Philadelphia: Pvt. ptd. at the University of Pennsylvania, 1939.

*Frenzel, H. *John Millington Synge's Work as a Contribution to Irish Folk-lore and to the Psychology of Primitive Tribes*. Bonn: n.p., 1932.

Gerstenberger, Donna Lorine. *John Millington Synge*. New York: Twayne, 1964.

Good, Maurice. *John Synge Comes Next*. Dublin: Dolmen; New York: Humanities, 1973.

Greene, David Herbert, and Edward M. Stephens. *J. M. Synge, 1871-1909*. New York: Macmillan, 1959.

Harmon, Maurice, editor. *J. M. Synge, Centenary Papers, 1971*. Dublin: Dolmen; New York: Humanities, 1972.

Howe, Percival P. *J. M. Synge: A critical study*. London: Secker, 1912.

Johnston, Denis. *John Millington Synge*. New York: Columbia University, 1965.

Lucas, Frank Laurence. *The Drama of Chekhov, Synge, Yeats and Pirandello*. London: Cassell, 1963.

Masefield, John. *John M. Synge: A few personal recollections, with bibliographical notes*. Churchtown, Dundrum: Cuala; New York: Macmillan, 1915.

Macmanus, M. J. *A Bibliography of Books Written by J. M. Synge*. Dublin: n.p., 1930.

Price, Alan Frederick. *Synge and Anglo-Irish Drama*. London: Methuen, 1961.

*Riva, Serafino. *La Tradizione celtica e la moderna letteratura irlandese. I. John Millington Synge*. Roma: n.p., 1937.

Setterquist, Jan Sigurd. *Ibsen and the Beginnings of Anglo Irish Drama: Part I. John Millington Synge*. Upsala: University of High Studies.

Shaw, Ruth. *John Synge's Aran*. New York: Devin-Adair (in prep.).

Skelton, Robin. *J. M. Synge*. (Irish Writer's Series). Lewisburg, Pa.: Bucknell University, 1972.

————. *J. M. Synge and His World.* New York: Viking, 1971.

————. *Remembering Synge. Dublin:* Dolmen, n.d.

————. *The Writings of J. M. Synge.* London: Thames & Hudson; New York: Bobbs, Merrill, 1971.

Strong, Leonard Alfred George. *John Millington Synge.* London: Allen and Unwin, 1941.

Synge, Samuel, M. D. *Letters to My Daughter: Memories of John Millington Synge.* Dublin and Cork: Talbot, 1932.

*Thorning, Just. *J. M. Synge. En moderne irsk dramatiker.* Kobenhavn: n.p., 1921.

Vaughan Williams, Ralph. *Riders to the Sea.* Set to music by R. V. Williams. London: Oxford Univ.; New York, C. Finc., c1936.

Whitaker, Thomas R., editor. *Twentieth Century Interpretations of the Playboy of the Western World.* Englewood Cliffs, N. J.: Prentice-Hall, 1969.

Yeats, William Butler. *The Death of Synge, and other passages from an old diary.* Dublin: Cuala, 1928.

————. *Synge and the Ireland of His Time.* With a note concerning a walk through Connemara with him by Jack Butler Yeats. Churchtown, Dundrum: Cuala, 1911.

Honor Tracy (1915-   )

FICTION

The Beauty of the World. London: Methuen, 1967.

The Butterflies of the Province. New York: Random House; London: Eyre Methuen, 1970.

The Deserters. London: Methuen, 1954.

The First Day of Friday. London: Methuen; New York: Random House, 1963.

Men at Work. London: Methuen; New York: Random House, 1967.

A Number of Things: A novel. London: Methuen; New York: Random, 1960.

The Prospects are Pleasing: A novel. London: Methuen; New York: Random House, 1958.

The Quiet End of Evening. New York: Random House; London: Eyre Methuen, 1972.

A Season of Mists: A novel. London: Methuen; New York: Random House, 1961.

Settled in Chambers: A novel. New York: Random House, c1967, 1968.

The Straight and Narrow Path. London: Methuen; New York: Random House, 1956.

NON-FICTION

Kakemono. *A sketchbook of post-war Japan.* London: Methuen, 1950.

Mind You, I've Said Nothing! Forays in the Irish Republic. London: Methuen, 1953.

Silk Hats and No Breakfast: Notes on a Spanish journey. London: Methuen, 1957. New York: Random House, c1957, 1958.

Spanish Leaves. London: Methuen; New York: Random House, 1964.

Winter in Castille. New York: Random House; London: Eyre Methuen, 1973.

TRANSLATED BY

Light, Barthelmy de. *The Conquest of Violence: An essay on war and revolution.* Trans. from the French text, rev. and enl. by the author. Intro. by Aldous Huxley. London: Routledge, 1937.

Katherine Tynan Hinkson (1861-1931)

COLLECTED AND SELECTED WORKS

Collected Poems. Fore. by George Russell. London: Macmillan, 1930.

Katherine Tynan. Intro. by Pamela Hinkson. London: Benn [1931].

Maxims from the Writings of Katherine Tynan. By the compiler of "Maxims from the Writings of Mgr. Benson." Elsie E. Marton. London: Washbourne, 1916.

Miracle Plays: Our Lord's Coming and Childhood. London: John Lane at the Bodley Head; Chicago: Stone and Kimball, 1895.

New Poems. London: Sidgwick and Jackson, 1911.

Poems. London: Lawrence and Bullen, 1901.

Poems of Katherine Tynan. Ed. with an intro. by Monk Gibbon. Dublin: Figgis, 1963; Chester Springs, Pa.: Dufour ,1966.

INDIVIDUAL WORKS

FICTION

Admirable Simmons. London and Melbourne: Ward, Lock, 1930.

Adventures of Alicia. London: White, 1906.

The Adventures of Carlo. London and Glasgow: Blackie [1900].

All for Love. London: Collins, 1932.

Betty Carew. London: Smith, Elder, 1910.

*Bitha's Wonderful Year, etc. London: Milford, 1921.

Briar Bush Maid. London and Melbourne: Ward, Lock, 1926.

Castle Perilous. London and Melbourne: Ward, Lock, 1928.

A Cluster of Nuts: Being sketches among my own people. London: Lawrence and Bullen, 1894.

Connor's Wood. London: Collins, 1933.

Countrymen All. London and Dublin: Maunsel, 1915.

Cousins and Others. London: Laurie [1909].

The Curse of Castle Eagle. New York: Duffield, 1915.

A Daughter of the Fields. London: Smith, Elder, 1900. Chicago: McClurg, [190?].

A Daughter of Kings. London: Nash; New York and Cincinnati: Benziger, 1905.

Daughter of the Manor. London: Blackie, 1914.

The Dear Irish Girl. London: Smith, Elder, 1899.

Dear Lady Bountiful. London: Ward, Lock, 1925.

Delia's Orchard. London and Melbourne: Ward, Lock, 1930.

Denise the Daughter. London and Melbourne: Ward, Lock, 1930.

Denys the Dreamer: A novel. London: Collins, 1920. New York and Cincinnati: Benziger, 1921.

Dick Pentreath. London: Smith, Elder, 1905. Chicago: McClurg, 1906.

The Face in the Picture. London and Melbourne: Ward, Lock, 1927.

Father Mathew. London: Macdonald and Evans; New York and Cincinnati: Benziger, 1908.

A Fine Gentleman. London and Melbourne: Ward, Lock, 1929.

The Forbidden Way. London: Collins, 1931.

For Maisie: A love story. London: Hodder and Stoughton, 1906.

For the White Rose. New York and Cincinnati: Benziger, 1905.

Fortune's Favorite: A novel. London: White, 1905.

Freda. London, New York, Toronto, and Melbourne: Cassell, 1910.

The French Wife. London: White; Philadelphia: Lippincott, 1904.

A Girl of Galway. London: Blackie, 1902.

The Golden Lily. New York and Cincinnati: Benziger, c1899, 1902.

The Golden Rose. London: Nash and Grayson, 1924. New York: Knopf, 1944.

Grayson's Girl. London: Collins, 1930.

The Great Captain: A story of the days of Sir Walter Raleigh. New York and Cincinnati: Benziger, 1902.

The Handsome Brandons: A story for girls. London: Blackie, 1899. Chicago: McClurg, 1900.

Handsome Quaker; and other stories. London: Bullen, 1902.

Haroun of London. London: Collins, 1927.

Heart o'Gold; or, the little princess: A story for girls. London: Partridge, 1912.

The Heiress of Wyke. London and Melbourne: Ward, Lock, 1926.

Her Father's Daughter: A novel. New York and Cincinnati: Benziger, c1900, 1901.

Her Ladyship. London: Smith, Elder, 1907. Chicago: McClurg, 1908.

Her Mother's Daughter. London: Smith, Elder, 1909.

Honey, My Honey. London: Smith, Elder, 1903.

The Honourable Molly. London: Smith, Elder, 1903.

The House. London: Collins, 1920.

The House in the Forest. London and Melbourne: Ward, Lock, 1928.

The House of the Crickets. London: Smith, Elder, 1908.

The House of Doom. London: Nash and Grayson, 1924.

The House of Dreams. London and Melbourne: Ward, Lock, 1934.

The House of the Foxes. London: Smith, Elder, 1915.

The House of the Secret. London: Clark, 1910.

The House on the Boggs. London and Melbourne: Ward, Lock, 1922.

The Infatuation of Peter. London: Collins, 1926.

The International Marriage. London and Melbourne: Ward, Lock, 1933.

An Isle in the Water: Short stories. London: Black; New York: Macmillan, 1896.

John-a-Dreams. London: Smith, Elder, 1916.

John Bulteel's Daughters. London: Smith, Elder, 1914.

Judy's Lovers. London: White, 1904.

Julia. London: Smith, Elder, 1904. Chicago: McClurg, 1905.

A King's Woman. London: Hurst and Blackett, 1902.

Kit. London: Smith, Elder, 1917.

Kitty Aubrey. London: Nisbit, 1909.

A Lad Was Born. Pref. note. London: Collins, 1934. Abr. ed., London: Mellifont, 1945.

The Land I Love Best. London: Ptd. at the Gresham for Unwin [1899].

Land of Mist and Mountains: Short stories. London: Unwin, 1895.

Led by a Dream; and other stories. London: n.p., 1899.

A Little Radiant Girl. London, Glasgow, and Bombay: Blackie, 1915.

A Lonely Maid. London and Melbourne: Ward, Lock, 1931.

The Lost Angel. London: Milne; Philadelphia: Lippincott, 1908.

Love of Brothers. London: Constable, 1919. New York and Cincinnati: Benziger, 1920.

Love of Sisters. London: Smith, Elder, 1902.

Lover of Women. London: Collins, 1928.

Lovers' Meeting. London: Laurie [1914].

Luck of the Fairfaxes: A story for girls. London, Glasgow, and New York: Collins, 1905.

A Mad Marriage. London: Collins, 1922.

The Man from Australia. London: Collins, 1919. Same with title *The Man from Australia: A passionate pilgrim*. London: Pub. for Collins by the National Book Co. [1931].

Margery Dawe. London: Blackie, 1916.

Mary Beaudesert, V. S. London: Collins, 1923.

Mary Gray. Paris, London, New York, Toronto, and Melbourne: Cassell, 1908. Abr. ed. in 1911.

Men and Maids. Dublin: Sealy, Bryers, and Walker, 1908.

Men, Not Angels; and other tales told to girls. London: Burns and Oates, 1914. New York: Kenedy, 1915.

A Mesalliance. New York: Duffield, 1913.

Midsummer Rose. London: Smith, Elder, 1913.

Miss Gascoigne. London: Murray, 1918.

Miss Mary. London: Murray, 1917.

Miss Phipps. London and Melbourne: Ward, Lock, 1925.

The Moated Grange. London: Collins, 1925. Abr. ed. with title *The Night of Terror*. London: Collins [1932].

Molly, My Heart's Delight. London: Smith, Elder, 1914.

The Most Charming Family. London and Melbourne: Ward, Lock, 1929.

Mrs. Pratt of Paradise Farm. See *Paradise Farm*.

My Love's But a Lassie. London, Melbourne, and Toronto: Ward, Lock, 1918.

The Night of Terror. See *The Moated Grange.*

Oh! What a Plague Is Love. London: Blackie, 1896. Chicago: McClurg, 1900.

The Other Man. London and Melbourne: Ward, Lock, 1932.

Paradise Farm. New York: Duffield, 1911. Same with principal character called Mrs. Pratt, not Mrs. Cripps, and with title *Mrs. Pratt of Paradise Farm.* London: Smith, Elder, 1913.

Pat. New York, Cincinnati, and Chicago: Benziger, 1913.

Pat the Adventurer. London and Melbourne: Ward, Lock, 1923.

Peggy, the Daughter. London, New York, Toronto, Melbourne: Cassell, 1909.

Philippa's Lover. London and Melbourne: Ward, Lock, 1931.

The Pitiful Lady. London and Melbourne: Ward, Lock, 1932.

The Playground. London and Melbourne: Ward, Lock, 1930.

Princess Katherine. New York: Duffield, c1910, 1911. London, Melbourne, and Toronto: Ward, Lock, 1912.

The Queen's Page: A story of the days of Charles I of England. New York, Cincinnati, and Chicago: Benziger, 1900.

The Rattlesnake. London: Ward, Lock, 1917.

A Red, Red Rose. London: Nash, 1903.

The Respectable Lady. London: Collins, 1927. New York: Appleton, 1928.

The Rich Man. London: Collins, 1929.

The River. London: Collins, 1929.

Rose of the Garden: The romance of Lady Sarah Lennox. London: Constable, 1912. Indianapolis: Bobbs-Merrill, 1913.

Sally Victrix. London: Collins, 1921.

The Second Wife; together with A July Rose. London: Murray, 1921.

A Shameful Inheritance. London, New York, Toronto, and Melbourne: Cassell, 1914.

She Walks in Beauty. London: Smith, Elder, 1899. Chicago: McClurg, 1900.

"Since I First Saw Your Face." London: Hutchinson, 1915.

The Squire's Sweetheart. London: Ward, Lock, 1915.

The Story of Bawn. London: Smith, Elder, 1906. Chicago: McClurg, 1907.

The Story of Cecilia. London: Smith, Elder; New York and Cincinnati: Benziger, 1911.

The Story of Clarice. London: Clarke, 1911.

The Story of Our Lord for Children. Dublin: Sealy, Bryers, and Walker, 1907. London: Burns, Oates, and Washbourne; New York and Cincinnati: Benziger, 1923.

That Sweet Enemy. London: Constable; Philadelphia: Lippincott, 1901.

They Loved Greatly. London: Nash and Grayson, 1923.

Three Fair Maids; or, The Burkes of Berrymoore. London: Blackie, 1901.

A Union of Hearts. London: Nisbit [1901].

The Way of a Maid. London: Lawrence and Bullen; New York: Dodd, Mead, 1895.

The Web of Fraulein. London, New York, and Toronto: Hodder and Stoughton, 1916.

The West Wind. London: Constable, 1916.

White Ladies. London: Nash and Grayson, 1922.

The Wild Adventure. London and Melbourne: Ward, Lock, 1927.

Wives: A novel. London: Hurst and Blackett [1924].

The Yellow Domino; and other stories. London: White, 1906.

AUTOBIOGRAPHY, BIOGRAPHY, AND CRITICISM BY

With Frances Maitland. *The Book of Flowers.* Intro. London: Smith, Elder, 1909.

A Dog Book. London: Hutchinson [1926].

Ireland. London: Blackie, 1909.

Katherine Tynan's Book of Irish History. Dublin and Belfast: Educational Co. of Ireland [1918].

Life in the Occupied Area. London: Hutchinson [1925].

A Little Book of Courtesies. Fore. London: Dent; New York: Dutton, 1906.

Lord Edward: A study in romance. London: Smith, Elder, 1916.

Memories. London: Nash and Grayson, 1924.

The Middle Years. London: Constable, 1916. Boston: Houghton, Mifflin, 1917.

A Nun, Her Friends and Her Order: Being a sketch of the life of Mother Mary Exaveria Fallon. London: Paul, Trench, Trübner, 1891.

O'Grady of Trinity: A story of university life. London: Lawrence and Bullen, 1896.

Twenty-five Years: Reminiscences. London: Smith, Elder; New York: Devin-Adair, 1913.

The Wandering Years. London: Constable; New York: Houghton, 1922.

The Years of Shadow. London: Constable; New York: Houghton, 1919.

POETRY

"Adveniat Regnum Tuum." New York: At the DeVinne Press for Fitz-Roy and Charlotte Carrington and their friends, Christmas 1908. 87 copies.

Ballads and Lyrics: Apologia. London: Paul, Trench, Trübner, 1891.

Cuckoo Songs. London: Mathews and Lane; Boston: Copeland and Day, 1894.

The Dearest of All. Portland, Maine: Ptd. for Thomas Mosher and pub. by him, 1910.

Evensong. Oxford: Blackwell, 1922.

Experiences. London: Bullen, 1908. 205 copies.

The Flower of Peace: A collection of devotional poetry. London: Burns and Oates, 1914. New York: Scribner's [1915].

The Flower of Youth: Poems in wartime. London: Sidgwick and Jackson, 1915.

Herb o' Grace: Poems in wartime. London: Sidgwick and Jackson, 1918.

The Holy War. London: Sidgwick and Jackson, 1916.

Innocencies: A book of verse. London: Bullen; Dublin: Maunsel, 1905.

Irish Poems. London: Sidgwick and Jackson, 1913. New York: Benziger, 1914.

Late Songs. London: Sidgwick and Jackson, 1917.

Lauds. London: Cedar, 1909. 350 copies.

A Little Book for John O'Mahoney's Friends. Intro. Petersfield: Pear Tree, 1906. 60 copies. Portland, Maine: Ptd. for Thomas Mosher and pub. by him, 1909.

A Little Book for Mary Gill's Friends. Intro. Petersfield: Pear Tree, 1906. 75 copies.

A Little Book of XXIV Carols. Portland, Maine: Ptd. for Thomas Mosher and pub. by him, 1907.

Louise de la Valliere; and other poems. London: Paul and Trench, 1885.

A Lover's Breast-knot. London: Mathews, 1928. 500 numbered copies.

A Memory. Portland, Maine: Ptd. for Thomas Mosher and pub. by him. 1910.

The Rhymed Life of St. Patrick. Fore. by Lt. Gen. Sir William Butler, G.C.B. London: Burns and Oates; New York and Cincinnati: Benziger, 1907.

Shamrock Song. San Francisco, 1939.

Shamrocks. London: Paul and Trench, 1887.

Shamrocks Over Ireland. San Francisco: Made for Albert M. Bender by Ansel Adams, St. Patrick's Day, 1939.

Twenty-one Poems. Sel. by W. B. Yeats. Dundrum: Dun Emer, 1907. 200 numbered copies.

Twilight Songs. Oxford: Blackwell; New York: Appleton, 1927.

The Wind in the Trees. A book of country verse. London: Richard, 1898.

EDITED BY

The Book of Memory: The birthday book of the blessed dead. Fore. London: Hodder and Stoughton [1906].

The Child at Prayer: A book of devotions for the young. Intro. London: Burns, Oates, and Washbourne, 1923.

Irish Love Songs. Pref. London: Unwin, 1892.

The Wild Harp: A selection from Irish poetry. Intro. London: Sidgwick and Jackson, 1913.

INTRODUCTIONS BY

Leamy, Edmund. *By the Barrow River; and other stories.* Dublin: Sealy, Bryers. 1907.

Longfellow, Henry Wadsworth. *Longfellow's Poems.* London: Dent; New York: Dutton, 1909.

Manning, Anne. *Mary Powell and Deborah's Diary.* London: Dent, New York: Dutton [1908].

Parry, Edith Ivor. *In the Garden of Childhood: An anthology of prose and verse for all child lovers, together with a tabulated journal for the insertion of various events in a child's life.* London: Routledge; New York: Dutton, 1913.

Read, Charles A. *The Cabinet of Irish Literature.* Sel. from the works of the chief poets, orators, and prose writers of Ireland. With biographical sketches and literary notices by Charles A. Read. Pref. Intro. 4 vols. London: Gresham, 1902, 1905. First pub. in 1879-80 without Tynan's pref.

Sigerson, Dorothy M. *The Sad Years.* Intro. London: Constable; New York: Doran, 1918.

Walsh, Michael. *Brown Earth and Green: Poems.* Dublin and Cork: Talbot, 1929.

Wynne, Frances. *Whisper! and other poems.* London: Mathews, 1908.

BIOGRAPHY AND CRITICISM

Rose, Marilyn G. *Katherine Tynan.* (Irish Writers Series). Lewisburg: Bucknell University, n.d.

William Butler Yeats (1865-1939)

BIBLIOGRAPHY

Cross, K. G. W. and Dunlop, R. T. *A Bibliography of Yeats Criticism, 1887-1965.* New York: Macmillan, 1972.

Stoll, John E. *The Great Deluge: A Yeats Bibliography.* Troy, N.Y.: Whitson, 1971.

Wade, Allan. *A Bibliography of the Writing of W. B. Yeats.* London: Hart-Davis, 1951. Rev. ed. in 1958. 3rd ed. in 1968.

RECENT PUBLICATIONS OF YEATS'S WRITINGS

The Byzantium Poems. Richard J. Finneran, editor. Columbus, Ohio: Merrill, 1970.

A Critical Edition of W. B. Yeats's John Sherman and Dhoya. Richard J. Finneran, editor. Detroit: Wayne State University, 1969.

Druid Craft: The Writing of The Shadowy Waters. Commentaries by Michael Sidnell, George Mayhew and David R. Clark. Amherst: University of Massachusetts, 1971.

Eleven Plays by William Butler Yeats. Ed. by A. Norman Jeffares. New York: Macmillan, 1968.

Fairy and Folk Tales of Ireland. With a foreword by Kathleen Raine. London: Colin Smythe, 1973. (Includes *Fairy and Folk Tales of the Irish Peasantry*, 1888, and *Irish Fairy Tales*, 1892.)

BIBLIOGRAPHICAL, BIOGRAPHICAL AND CRITICAL STUDIES ABOUT

Adams, Hazard. *Blake and Yeats: The Contrary Vision.* Ithaca, N.Y.: Cornell University, 1955.

Albright, Daniel. *The Myth Against Myth: A Study of Yeats's Imagination in Old Age.* New York and London: Oxford University, 1972.

Aldington, Richard. *A. E. Housman and W. B. Yeats: Two lectures.* Hurst, Berkshire: Peacocks, 1955. 350 copies.

Bachchan, Harbans Rai. *W. B. Yeats and Occultism: A study of his works in relation to Indian lore, the Cabbala, Swedenborg, Boehme and Theosophy.* Delhi: Motilal Barsidass, 1965.

Bayley, John. *The Romantic Survival*. London: Constable, 1957.

Berryman, C. *W. B. Yeats*. New York: Exposition, 1967.

Beum, Robert L. *The Poetic Art of William Butler Yeats*. New York: Ungar, 1969.

Bjersby, Birgit Maria Hermine (Johannsson). *The Interpretation of the Cuchulain Legend in the Works of W. B. Yeats*. Dublin: Hodges, Figgis; Upsala: A.-B. Lundequestska Bokhandeln; Cambridge, Mass.: Harvard University, 1951.

Black, Hester M. *William Butler Yeats: A Catalog of an exhibition from the P. S. O'Hegarty Collection in the University of Kansas Library*. Lawrence: University of Kansas Library, 1958.

Bloom, Harold. *Yeats*. New York: Oxford University, 1970.

Bornstein, George J. *Yeats and Shelley*. Chicago: University of Chicago, 1970.

Bose, Abinash C. *Three Mystic Poets: A Study of W. B. Yeats, A. E. and Rabindranath Tagore*. With an intro. by J. H. Cousins. Kolhapur School and Study Bookstore; Folcroft, Pa.: Folcroft Library Editions, 1945.

Bradford, Curtis B., ed. *W. B. Yeats: The Writing of the Player Queen*. DeKalb: Northern Illinois University (in prep.).

Bradford, Curtis B. *Yeats at Work*. Carbondale: Southern Illinois University, 1965.

Braun, John Theodore. *The Apostrophic Gesture*. The Hague: Mouton, 1971.

Bushrui, S. B. *Yeats's Verse Plays: The revisions, 1900-1910*. Oxford: Clarendon, 1965.

Chaterjee, Bhabatosh. *The Poetry of W. B. Yeats*. Bombay: Orient Longmans, 1962.

Clark, David R. *The Poetry of W. B. Yeats*. London: Longmans, 1962.

———. *W. B. Yeats and the Theatre of Desolate Reality*. Dublin: Dolmen, 1965.

Cowell, Raymond, compiler. *Critics on Yeats*. London: Allen and Unwin; Coral Gables: University of Miami, 1971.

Cowell, Raymond. *W. B. Yeats*. London: Evans Bros., 1969. New York: Arco, 1970.

Davis, Edward. *Yeats' Early Contacts with French Poetry.* Pretoria: University of South Africa, 1961.

Davis, Robert Bernard. *The Shaping of an Agate: A story of the development of the literary theory of W. B. Yeats from 1885-1910.* Chicago: Library Department of Photographic Reproduction, University of Chicago, 1956.

Day Lewis, Cecil. *Notable Images of Virtue: Emily Brontë, George Meredith, W. B. Yeats.* Toronto: Ryerson, 1954.

Desai, Rupin W. *Yeats's Shakespeare.* Evanston: Northwestern University, 1971.

The Dolmen Press Yeats Centenary Papers. Dublin: Dolmen, 1965. No. 1. Malins, Edward. *Yeats and the Easter Rising.* 2. Lister, Raymond. *Beulah to Byzantium: A study of the parallels in the works of W. B. Yeats, Samuel Palmer, and Edward Calvert.* 3. Alspach, Russell K. *Yeats and Innisfree.* 4. Telfer, Giles W. L. *Yeats's Idea of the Gael.* 5. Faulkner, Peter. *Yeats and the Irish Eighteenth Century.* 6. Ishibashi, Hiro. *Yeats and the Noh: Types of Japanese beauty and their reflection in Yeats's plays.* Ed. by Anthony Kerrigan. 7. Saul, George Brandon. *In . . . Luminous Wind.* 8. Bradford, Curtis, *Yeats's 'Last Poems' Again.* 9. Harper, George Mills. *Yeats's Quest for Eden.* 10. *Yeats and Patrick McCarton. A Fenian Friendship: Letters with a commentary by John Unterecker and an address on Yeats the Fenian by Patrick McCarton.* 11. Ellmann, Richard. *Yeats and Joyce.* Same in one volume. Dublin: Dolmen; London: Oxford University; Chester Springs: Dufour, 1968. 850 copies signed by the editor.

Domville, Eric, editor. *A Concordance to the Plays of W. B. Yeats.* 2 vols. London and Ithaca, N.Y.: Cornell University, 1972.

Donoghue, Denis, ed. *The Integrity of Yeats.* Cork: Mercier, 1964.

———. *William Butler Yeats.* London: Fontana; New York: Viking, 1971.

Dougan, R. O., compiler. *W. B. Yeats: Manuscripts and Printed Books.* Dublin: Ptd. for the Friends of the Library of Trinity College, Dublin, by Colm Ó Lochlainn at the Sign of the Three Candles, 1956.

Dougherty, Adelyn. *Study of Rhythmic Structure in the Verse of William Butler Yeats.* De Proprietatibus Litterarum. Series Practica, Vol. 38. The Hague: Mouton; New York: Humanities, 1973.

Durkan, Michael J. *William Butler Yeats: 1865-1965.* A catalogue of his works and associated items in Olin Library, Wesleyan University. Essay by David R. Clark. Middletown, Conn.: Wesleyan University, 1965.

Duryee, Mary Ballard. *Words Alone are Certain Good. William Butler Yeats: Himself, the Poet, His Ghost.* Dublin: Dolmen, 1961. London: Oxford University, 1962.

Eddins, Dwight. *Yeats: The Nineteenth Century Matrix.* University, Ala.: University of Alabama, 1971.

Ellmann, Richard. *Eminent Domain; Yeats among Wilde, Joyce, Pound, Eliot, and Auden.* London and New York: Oxford University, 1967.

———. *The Identity of Yeats.* London: Macmillan; New York: Oxford University, 1954.

———. *Yeats: The Man and the Masks.* New York: Macmillan, 1948. London: Macmillan, 1949.

———. *Yeats and Joyce.* Dublin: Dolmen; London: Oxford University, 1967.

Engleberg, Edward. *The Vast Design: Patterns in W. B. Yeats's Aesthetic.* Toronto: University of Toronto, 1964.

Frazer, George Sutherland. *W. B. Yeats.* London and New York: Pub. for the British Council by Longmans, Green, 1954.

Garab, Arra M. *Beyond Byzantium.* DeKalb: Northern Illinois, 1969.

Gibbon, Monk. *The Masterpiece and the Man: Yeats as I knew him.* London: Hart-Davis; New York: Macmillan, 1959.

*Gilbert, Sandra. *The Poetry of W. B. Yeats.* Monarch Literature Notes on the Poetry of Yeats. New York: Monarch, 1965.

Gill, S. M. *Six Symbolist Plays of Yeats.* New Delhi, India: S. Chand, 1971.

Gogarty, Oliver St. John. *William Butler Yeats: A Memoir.* With a pref. by Myles Dillon. Dublin: Dolmen, 1963.

Gordon, Donald James. *W. B. Yeats: Images of a Poet.* With contributions by Ian Fletcher, Frank Kermode and Robin Skelton. Manchester: Manchester University, 1961. New York: Barnes & Noble, 1962.

*Green, M. B. *Yeats's Blessings on Von Hügel.* London: Longmans; New York: Norton, 1968.

Grossman, Allen R. *Poetic Knowledge in the Early Yeats.* Charlottesville: University Press of Virginia, 1969.

Guhu, Naresh. *W. B. Yeats: An Indian Approach.* Calcutta: Jadaupur University, 1968.

Gurd, Patty. *The Early Poetry of William Butler Yeats.* Lancaster, Pa.: New Era Printing Co., 1916.

Gwynn, Stephen Lucius, ed. *Scattering Branches: Tributes to the Memory of W. B. Yeats.* London: Macmillan, 1940.

Gwynn, Stephen Lucius. *William Butler Yeats.* Port Washington, N.Y.: Kennikat, 1965.

Hall, James, and Steinmann, Martin. *The Permanence of Yeats.* Selected criticism. New York: Macmillan, 1950.

Hanley, Mary. *Thoor Ballylee—Home of William Butler Yeats.* Liam Miller, ed. Dublin: Dolmen, 1965.

Harper, George M. *Yeats's Golden Dawn.* New York: Barnes & Noble, 1974.

Harris, Daniel A. *Yeats: Coole Park and Ballylee.* Baltimore: Johns Hopkins University, 1974.

Henn, Thomas Rice. *The Lonely Tower: Studies in the poetry of W. B. Yeats.* London: Methuen, 1950. New York: Pellegrini and Cudahy, 1952.

Hoare, Dorothy M. *The Works of Morris and Yeats in Relation to Early Saga Literature.* Cambridge: Cambridge University; New York: Macmillan, 1937.

Hoffman, Daniel B. *Barbarous Knowledge.* London and New York: Oxford University, 1967.

Hone, Joseph Maunsel. *W. B. Yeats, 1865-1939.* London: Macmillan, 1942. New York: Macmillan, 1943.

Hone, Joseph Maunsel. *William Butler Yeats: The poet in contemporary Ireland.* Dublin and London: Maunsel, 1916.

*Huttemann, Gerta. *Wesen der Dichtung und Aufgabe des Dichters bei William Butler Yeats.* Bonn: n. p., 1929.

Jeffares, A. Norman. *The Circus Animals.* London: Macmillan; Stanford: Stanford University, 1970.

————. *A Commentary on the Collected Poems of W. B. Yeats.* London: Macmillan; Stanford: Stanford University, 1968.

————. *The Poetry of W. B. Yeats.* Great Neck, N.Y.: Barron's Educational Series, 1961.

————. *W. B. Yeats, Man and Poet.* London: Routledge and Paul; New Haven: Yale University, 1949.

————. *William Butler Yeats: Selected Criticism.* London: Macmillan, 1965.

————. and Cross, W. K. G., eds. *In Excited Reverie.* London and New York: Macmillan, 1965.

Jochum, K. P. S. *W. B. Yeats's Plays.* Saarbrücken: Universitat de Saarlandes Anglistisches Institut, 1966.

John, Brian. *Supreme Fictions: Studies in the Works of William Blake, Thomas Carlyle, W. B. Yeats and D. H. Lawrence.* London and Montreal: McGill-Queens University, 1974.

Jones, James Land. *Adam's Dream: Mythic Consciousness in Keats and Yeats.* Athens, Ga.: University of Georgia, 1975.

*Kansas University Libraries. *William Butler Yeats.* Folcroft, Pa.: Folcroft Library Editions, 1973.

Keane, Patrick J., ed. *William Butler Yeats.* New York: McGraw-Hill, 1973.

Kirby, Sheela. *The Yeats Country.* A guide to places in the west of Ireland associated with the life and writings of William Butler Yeats. Dublin: Dolmen, 1962.

Kleinstuck, Johannes Walter. *W. B. Yeats; oder, Der Dichter in der modernen Welt.* Hamburg: Leibniz-Verlag, 1963.

Koch, Vivienne. *W. B. Yeats. The Tragic Phase: A Study of the Last Poems.* London: Routledge and Paul, 1951. Baltimore: Johns Hopkins University, 1952.

Krans, Horatio Sheafe. *William Butler Yeats and the Irish Literary Revival.* New York: McClure, 1904. London: Heinemann, 1905.

Kremen, Kathryn R. *The Imagination of the Resurrection.* Lewisburg, Pa.: Bucknell University, 1972.

Lai, P., trans. *The Isa Upanisad.* With an essay on the difficulties of translation, based on a study of the Yeats-Purohit version of the Isa-Upanisad. Calcutta: Writers Workshop, 1968.

*Lentriccia, F. *The Gaiety of Language: An essay on the radical poetics of W. B. Yeats and Wallace Stevens*. Berkeley: University of California, 1968.

Levine, Bernard. *The Dissolving Image*. Detroit: Wayne State University, 1970.

Lucas, Frank Laurence. *The Drama of Chekhov, Yeats, Synge and Pirandello*. London: Cassell, 1963.

MacLeish, Archibald. *Yeats and the Belief in Life*. An address at the University of New Hampshire, January 17, 1957. Durham: University of New Hampshire, 1958.

MacLiammhóir, Micheál, and Boland, Eavan. *W. B. Yeats and His World*. London: Thames and Hudson, 1971. New York: Viking, 1972.

MacNeice, Louis. *The Poetry of W. B. Yeats*. London: Oxford University, 1941. Same with a fore. by Richard Ellmann. London: Faber and Faber, 1967.

Malins, Edward. *A Preface to Yeats*. New York: Scribner, 1975.

Marcus, Phillip L. *Yeats and the Beginning of the Irish Renaissance*. London and Ithaca, N.Y.: Cornell University, 1970.

Masefield, John. *Some Memories of W. B. Yeats*. Dublin: Cuala, 1940. 385 numbered copies.

Maxwell, Desmond Ernest Stewart, and Bushrui, S. B., eds. *W. B. Yeats, 1865-1939*. Centenary Essays on the Art of W. B. Yeats. Ibadan, Nigeria: Ibadan University, 1965.

Mayhew, Joyce. *Ad multos annos: W. B. Yeats in his seventieth year*. Oakland: Bender, 1935.

Meir, Colin. *The Ballads and Songs of W. B. Yeats: The Anglo-Irish Heritage in Subject and Style*. New York: Barnes & Noble, 1974.

Melchiori, Giorgio. *The Whole Mystery of Art: Pattern into poetry in the work of W. B. Yeats*. London: Routledge and Paul, 1960. New York: Macmillan, c1960, 1961.

Menon, V. K. Narayana. *The Development of William Butler Yeats*. London and Edinburgh: Oliver and Boyd, 1942. Rev. ed., 1960.

Misra, B. P. *W. B. Yeats*. Allahabad: Kital-Mahal, 1962.

Mokashi, R. S. *The Later Phase in the Development of W. B. Yeats*. Dharkar, India: Karnatak University, 1966.

Moore, John Rees. *Masks of Love and Death.* London and Ithaca, N.Y.: Cornell University, 1971.

Moore, Virginia. *The Unicorn: William Butler Yeats' search for reality.* New York: Macmillan, 1954.

Nathan, Leonard E. *The Tragic Drama of William Butler Yeats: Figures in a dance.* New York and London: Columbia University, 1965.

New Yeats Papers. Dublin: Dolmen Press, 1971-1974. (Dist. by Oxford University Press outside of Ireland and U.S.A., by Humanities Press in U.S.A.). I. Murphy, William M. *The Yeats Family and the Pollexfens of Sligo.* With drawings by John Butler Yeats. II. Raine, Kathleen. *Yeats, The Tarot and The Golden Dawn.* III. *W. B. Yeats and the Designing of Ireland's Coinage.* Texts by W. B. Yeats and Others, with an intro. by Brian Cleeve. IV. Finneran, Richard J. *The Prose Fiction of W. B. Yeats: The Search for 'Those Simple Forms.'* V. White, James. *John Butler Yeats and the Irish Renaissance.* With pictures from the collection of Michael Butler Yeats and from the National Collections of Ireland. VI. Harper, George M. *Go Back Where You Belong: Yeats's Return from Exile.* VII. Miller, Liam. *The Dun Emer Press, Later the Cuala Press.* VIII. Raine, Kathleen. *Life in Death and Death in Life: Cuchulain Comforted and News for the Delphic Oracle.* (Further papers, issues IX to XII, will be announced later).

No author. *Some Critical Appreciations of William Butler Yeats as Poet, Orator and Dramatist.* N. p., n. d.

O'Connor, Ulick, ed. *The Yeats We Knew.* New York: British Book Center, 1971.

O'Donnell, James Preston. *Sailing to Byzantium: A study in the development of the later style and symbolism in the poetry of W. B. Yeats.* Cambridge: Harvard University, 1939.

Orel, Harold. *The Development of William Butler Yeats: 1885-1900.* Lawrence: The University of Kansas Publications, 1968.

Oshima, Shotaro. *Jeitsu Kenkyu. W. B. Yeats: A Study.* Tokyo: Taibunska, 1927.

———. *W. B. Yeats.* Tokyo: Kenkyasha, 1934.

———. *W. B. Yeats: The Later Poetry.* Pref. London: Cambridge;

Parish, Stephen M. *A Concordance to the Poems of W. B. Yeats.* Ithaca, N.Y.: Cornell University, 1963.

Parkinson, Thomas F. *W. B. Yeats, Self Critic: A study of his early verse*. Berkeley: University of California; London: Cambridge University, 1951.

————. *W. B. Yeats: The Later Poetry*. Pref. London: Cambridge; Berkeley and Los Angeles: University of California, 1964.

Perloff, Marjorie C. *Rhyme and Meaning in the Poetry of Yeats*. The Hague: Mouton, 1970.

Pollock, J. H. *William Butler Yeats*. Dublin: Talbot; London: Duckworth, 1935.

Pritchard, William H., editor. *W. B. Yeats: A Critical Anthology*. Harmondsworth: Penguin, 1972.

Rajan, Balachandra. *W. B. Yeats: A critical introduction*. London: Hutchinson; New York: Hillary, 1965.

Rattray, R. F. *Poets in the Flesh: Tagore, Yeats, Dunsany, Stephens, Drinkwater*. Cambridge: Golden Head, 1961.

Reid, Benjamin Lawrence. *William Butler Yeats: The lyric of tragedy*. Norman: University of Oklahoma, 1961.

Reid, Forest. *W. B. Yeats: A critical study*. London: Secker, 1915.

Ronsley, Joseph. *Yeats's Autobiography: Life as symbolic pattern*. Harvard University, 1968.

Roth, William M. *A Catalogue of English and American First Editions of William Butler Yeats*. Prepared for an exhibition of his works held in the Yale University Library beginning May 15, 1939. New Haven: Yale, 1939.

Rudd, Margaret. *Divided Image: A study of William Blake and W. B. Yeats*. London: Routledge and Paul, 1953.

Ryan, Rosalie, Sister. *Symbolic Elements in the Plays of William Butler Yeats, 1892-1921*. Washington, D.C. Catholic University of America, 1952.

Salvadori, Corinna. *Yeats and Castiglione: Poet and Courtier*. A study of some fundamental concepts in the philosophy and poetic creed of W. B. Yeats in the light of Castiglione's *Il Libro del Cortegiano*. Dublin: Figgis; New York: Barnes and Noble, 1965.

Saul, George Brandon. *Prolegomena to the Study of Yeats's Plays*. Philadelphia: University of Pennsylvania, 1957.

————. *Prolegomena to the Study of Yeats's Poems.* Philadelphia: University of Pennsylvania, 1958.

Schweishut, Elizabeth. *Yeats' Feendichtung.* Darmstadt: Bender, 1927.

Seiden, Morton Irving. *William Butler Yeats: The poet as a myth maker, 1865-1939.* East Lansing: Michigan State University, 1962.

Shaw, Priscilla. *Rilke, Valéry and Yeats: The Domain of the Self.* New Brunswick, New Jersey: Rutgers University, 1964.

Skelton, Robin, and Ann Saddlemyer (eds.). *The World of W. B. Yeats: Essays in Perspective.* Dublin: Dolmen; Seattle: University of Washington; Victoria, British Columbia: Adelphi Bookshop for the University of Victoria, 1965. Rev. ed. in 1967 by the University of Washington.

Smith, Arthur James Marshall. *Poet Young and Old: W. B. Yeats.* Toronto: University of Toronto, 1939.

Snukal, Robert. *High Talk: The Philosophical Poetry of W. B. Yeats.* Cambridge and New York: Cambridge University, 1973.

Spivak, G. C. *Myself I Must Remake.* New York: Crowell-Collier, 1974.

Stallworthy, Jon. *Between the Lines: Yeats's poetry in the making.* Oxford: Clarendon, 1963.

————. *Vision and Revision in Yeats' Last Poems.* London and New York: Oxford University, 1969.

————. *Yeats: Last Poems.* London: Macmillan, 1968. Nashville: Aurora Publishers, 1970.

Starkie, Walter Fitzwilliam, and A. Norman Jeffares. *Homage to Yeats, 1865-1965.* Papers read at a Clark Library Seminar, October 16, 1965. Intro. by Majl Ewing. Los Angeles: William Andrews Clark Memorial Library, University of California, 1966.

Stauffer, Donald A. *The Golden Nightingale.* Essays on some principles of poetry in the lyrics of W. B. Yeats. New York: Macmillan, 1949.

Stock, Amy Geraldine. *W. B. Yeats: His Poetry and Thought.* Cambridge: Cambridge University, 1961.

Strong, L. A. G. *A Letter to W. B. Yeats.* London: Leonard and Virginia Woolf at the Hogarth, 1932.

Symons, Arthur J. A. *A Bibliography of the First Editions of Books by William Butler Yeats*. London: The First Editions Club, 1924. 500 numbered copies.

Tindall, William York. *W. B. Yeats*. New York: Columbia University, 1966.

Torchiana, Donald T. *W. B. Yeats and Georgian Ireland*. Evanston, Ill.: Northwestern University; London: Oxford University, 1966.

Ueda, Makoto. *Zeami, Basho, Yeats, Pound: A study in Japanese and English poetics*. The Hague: Mouton, 1965.

Unterecker, John Eugene. *A Reader's Guide to William Butler Yeats*. New York: Noonday, 1959.

————. (ed.). *Yeats: A collection of critical essays*. Englewood Cliffs, N.J.: Prentice-Hall, 1963.

Ure, Peter. *Towards a Mythology: Studies in the poetry of W. B. Yeats*. Liverpool: University of Liverpool, 1946.

————. *Yeats*. Edinburgh and London: Oliver and Boyd, 1963. Pub. in the U.S.A. with title *W. B. Yeats*. New York: Grove, 1964.

————. *Yeats and Anglo-Irish Literature*. New York: Harper and Row, 1974.

————. *Yeats, the Playwright*. A commentary on character and design in the major plays. London: Routledge and Paul; New York: Barnes and Noble, 1963.

Vendler, Helen Hennessey. *Yeats's Vision and The Later Plays*. London: Oxford University; Cambridge: Harvard University, 1963.

Wade, Allan. *A Bibliography of the Writings of William Butler Yeats*. Stratford-on-Avon: Shakespeare Head, 1908. 60 numbered copies.

Webster, Brenda S. *Yeats*. Stanford: Stanford University, 1973. Also titled *Yeats: A psychoanalytic study*. London: Macmillan, 1973.

Wellesley College Library. *William Butler Yeats at Wellesley*. Note by Hannnah Dustin French. Middletown, Conn.: The Friends of the Wellesley College Library, 1952.

Whitaker, Thomas R. *Swan and Shadow: Yeats dialogue with history*. Chapel Hill: University of North Carolina, 1964.

Whitworth Art Gallery. *W. B. Yeats: Images of a poet*. Exhibition Catalogue. Fore. Whitworth Art Gallery, University of Manchester, 1961.

Wilson, Francis Alexander Charles Cauvin. *W. B. Yeats and Tradition.* London: Gollancz; New York: Macmillan, 1958.

———. *Yeats's Iconography.* London: Gollancz; New York: Macmillan, 1960.

Winters, Yvor. *The Poetry of W. B. Yeats.* Denver: A. Swallow, 1960.

Wren, C. L. *W. B. Yeats: A literary study.* London: Marby, 1920.

Zwerdling, Alex. *Yeats and The Heroic Ideal.* New York: New York University, 1965.

Compilers

Frank L. Kersnowski received his B.A. (1957) and M.A. (1959) from The University of Tennessee and his Ph.D. (1963) from The University of Kansas. His professional interest in Irish studies began in 1960 when he became a member of the American Committee for Irish Studies. His publications include *John Montague* (Bucknell, 1975) and *The Outsiders: Poets of Contemporary Ireland* (T.C.U., 1975) as well as articles in various journals. He is professor of English at Trinity University, San Antonio.

C. W. Spinks, assistant professor of English, joined the faculty of Trinity University in 1970 as a specialist in nineteenth century British literature. He received his B.A. (1964) from Wayland Baptist College in Texas and his M.A. (1965) and Ph.D. (1970) from The University of Nebraska. He has published articles on Blake, Shaw, and science fiction.

Laird Loomis received his B.A. (1967) and his M.A. (1975) from Trinity University. He is presently teaching in San Antonio.